NATHAN A. HUGHES, ESQ.

TO LIVE CHRIST, TO DIE GAIN

Matthew Henry

Every blessing

P. H. Sam

Oct, 2018.

Matthew Henry

by

Philip Henry Eveson

EP BOOKS

1st Floor Venture House, 6 Silver Court, Watchmead,
Welwyn Garden City, UK, AL7 1TS

www.epbooks.org
sales@epbooks.org

EP BOOKS are distributed in the USA by:
JPL Fulfillment
3741 Linden Avenue Southeast,
Grand Rapids, MI 49548.

E-mail: sales@jplfulfillment.com
Tel: 877.683.6935

First published 2012

Reprinted 2016

British Library Cataloguing in Publication Data available

ISBN: 978–0–85234–799–7

Unless otherwise indicated, all Scripture quotations are taken from the Holy Bible, Authorized (King James) Version.

Printed and bound in the UK by 4edge Limited

To my four grandchildren
Joshua, Nia, Hannah and Joseph

Contents

Timeline

1689	Matthew's first child, Katharine, born; death of his wife
1690	Marries Mary Warburton
1691	Elizabeth born
1692	Death of Elizabeth
1693	Birth and death of Mary
1694	Esther born
1696	Death of Matthew's father, Philip Henry
1697	Ann born
1698	Death of Ann
1700	Philip born; new chapel building opened
1701	Act of Settlement; Elizabeth born
1703	Sarah born
1706	First volume of his *Bible Exposition* published
1706/1707	Acts of Union between the English and Scottish Parliaments
1708	Theodosia born; second volume of *Bible Exposition* published
1710	Third volume of his *Bible Exposition* and *A Method for Prayer* published
1711	Mary born; the Occasional Conformity Act
1712	Commences his ministry in Hackney; fourth volume of his *Bible Exposition* published

1714   Last visit to Chester and death; Schism Act; death
        of Queen Anne

1721   Fifth volume of his *Bible Exposition* published
        posthumously

Preface

When I was asked to consider contributing to this Bitesize series I had no difficulty in choosing Matthew Henry from the list of names on offer. A lovely set of Matthew Henry's commentaries on the New Testament was displayed prominently in the bookcase of our living room when I was a child, so it was the first commentary I ever consulted as a young man. My father was a blacksmith, but as a Christian he was always eager to share his faith with his workmates. One of them invited us to his home one evening to see whether we were interested in some old books he had in the cellar. To my amazement there was a whole set of the Puritan Thomas Goodwin's works and a large gilded family Bible with illustrated plates. The Bible, unusually, contained only the Old Testament text, but with Matthew Henry's comments. We had some difficulty walking home with these prized possessions, but it was worth the effort.

It was not long before I realized that Matthew Henry was from my part of the world. I come from a village outside Wrexham. Matthew Henry was born and brought up only a few miles from where I lived, and ministered for most of his life a mere eleven miles from Wrexham. This encouraged me to find out more about him.

During my teenage years I was not too happy with my middle name, Henry, as it was out of fashion at the time and I was often ribbed at school over it. Later, I came to be proud of it when I learned more of Matthew Henry's father, Philip Henry, even though I was not named after him.

It has been a privilege and a humbling experience researching the life and ministry of this wonderful man of God, his family background and his many friends. I pray that the life of Matthew Henry that this Philip Henry has 'fathered' will help to further the memory of an outstanding minister of the gospel and stimulate more people to read at least his most easily accessible books (which can be purchased, borrowed or downloaded).

Introduction

The name of Matthew Henry will always be associated with his famous commentary. All over the world there are Christians who still appreciate the value of his work. For three hundred years his exposition of the biblical text, devotional comments, practical wisdom, warm theology and helpful insights have been of immense value to Christians both in their private devotions and family worship. Preachers and teachers of God's Word have also found his work a useful tool in the preparation of their sermons and Scripture lessons. Matthew Henry died aged fifty-one, greatly respected during his life for his preaching, wise counsel and published works. Since then his catechism and advice on prayer, as well as his popular commentary, have been a source of spiritual nourishment to many.

Matthew Henry lived during a very difficult period for Christians who were not prepared to submit by order of the state to Anglican worship and organization. They were treated as second-class citizens and were often unjustly accused of sedition. The dates of Matthew Henry's life span the years when there was sustained official persecution; and even when the position of the Dissenters, or Nonconformists as they came to be called, eased after the bloodless Revolution of 1688, they were still treated with suspicion. Bills in Parliament continued to be formulated to curb their freedoms until the year of Matthew's death, 1714, when Tory power and Stuart dynasty gave way to Whig ascendancy and the Hanoverian succession.

In order to appreciate more clearly the situation in which Matthew Henry grew up and later ministered, it is necessary to say more than usual about his father and the circumstances of the time.

1

Background

Dates like 1066 stand out and are long remembered. 1662 is another such year, especially for non-Anglicans. It was the year that the Act of Uniformity was passed, causing some two thousand ministers of the gospel in England and Wales to be removed from the people they served and prevented from exercising their God-given callings as gospel ministers. It is often referred to as the 'Great Ejection'. But as every dark cloud has a silver lining, so this grim year for many godly preachers was the year in which Matthew Henry was born. God would use him not only as a gospel preacher to his own generation but for the spiritual benefit of succeeding generations of Christians.

Matthew's father, Philip Henry, lived in Worthenbury, a village in North-East Wales lying seven miles south-east of Wrexham on the road between Bangor-on-Dee (the Welsh form is Bangor-is-y-coed) and Malpas in Cheshire. At that time the whole area east of the River Dee to the English border and known as Maelor Saesneg ('English Maelor') belonged to a detached part of Flintshire. It is now part of the county borough of Wrexham and remains by and large a farming community with some Henry descendants still living in the vicinity. Life in the village was dominated by the Puleston family, who had resided at nearby Emral Hall (demolished in 1936) since the thirteenth century. The area was not immune from the effects of the Civil War. First the king's forces were billeted at the Hall and then in 1644 supporters of Parliament. Sir John Puleston had been a judge; and among his other responsibilities during Cromwell's rule he was a member of the Commission for the Propagation of the Gospel in Wales (1650). It was said of him that in renewing leases on the estate Sir John substituted for the customary obligation of keeping a hound or hawk for the landlord that of keeping a Bible in the house. His wife Elizabeth was a godly lady and sympathetic to the Puritan cause. It was into this family that Matthew's father came in 1653, aged only twenty-two, having graduated B.A. (1651) and M.A. (1652) at Christchurch, Oxford, where the great theologian John Owen was the College Dean and Vice-Chancellor of the University.

Philip Henry's duties included officiating at family worship, tutoring the Puleston sons and preaching at Worthenbury church. This church, a parochial chapel, belonged originally to the parish of Bangor-is-y-coed (not to be confused with the cathedral city of Bangor near Anglesey), an ancient Celtic monastic site where, according to the Venerable Bede, twelve hundred monks were slaughtered by the Anglo-Saxons for not conforming to the pope's wishes. In 1658, through the efforts of Sir John, the chapel was separated from Bangor. Worthenbury became a parish in its own right and Philip was formally and legally appointed as the officiating minister following his ordination the previous year. His patron even built him 'a very handsome house.'

Unfortunately for Philip Henry, Lady Elizabeth died in 1658

and her husband the following year. Their eldest son and heir, Roger Puleston, did not follow in the godly footsteps of his parents and made life more difficult for Philip. This rebellious teenager had resented the presence of his godly tutor from the moment he had stepped into their home. His pride had also been hurt from a hard smack across the face that Henry had given him when Roger assaulted him. Philip regretted the incident, knowing that the whole situation had been mismanaged.

Although Philip Henry welcomed the return of the monarchy in 1660 with Charles II proclaimed king, and took the oath of allegiance in November 1660, there were indications that his legally secure situation at Worthenbury was under threat. He had resisted a call to become the minister of the parish church at Wrexham in 1659, a town larger than Cardiff or Swansea at that time, as well as another situation in London soon after, believing it to be his duty to remain where God had placed him.

Philip Henry was a Presbyterian who believed, like the Anglicans, in a national church, the parish system and a hierarchical church government. He had been ordained after a long delay in 1657 by Presbyterian ministers in North Shropshire according to rules drawn up by the Westminster Assembly (1643–1649). But as a convinced Presbyterian Philip Henry did not believe in episcopacy (rule by bishops). Neither did he see any need to be re-ordained by a bishop; nor that items not directed by the New Testament should be made compulsory (such as the Anglican *Book of Common Prayer*, clerical robes, kneeling at the communion rail and baptizing with the sign of the cross). During the time of the Civil Wars and the Commonwealth period under Oliver Cromwell, there had been much freedom of worship. With the return of the King, early hopes of liberty of conscience in matters of religion were soon dashed by the Cavalier Parliament. Robert Fogg, the minister of

Bangor-on-Dee from 1646 to 1660, was put out of his parish by
the Bill for Settling Ministers and the former incumbent, Henry
Bridgeman, was reinstated. The culmination of the process of
restoring the state church to its former position came with the
royal assent being given to the Act of Uniformity in May 1662.
Every minister was required to declare publicly his approval
of everything contained in the *Book of Common Prayer* before
St. Batholomew's Day (24 August 1662). All who declined to
conform would be automatically deprived of their livings. In
other words, they would be put out of the churches where they
ministered and forced to vacate their vicarages and rectories.
The Act also applied to university lecturers and fellows, and to
schoolmasters.

Thus Philip Henry found himself among about 130 other
men in Wales who were silenced during this period of restoring
the old order. Philip had endeavoured to gain the friendship of
Bridgeman, who quickly repossessed the Worthenbury church,
as all ecclesiastical transactions during the interregnum were
declared null and void. (By act of Parliament it again became a
separate parish in 1689 and has remained so ever since.) It meant
that Philip became, in effect, Bridgeman's curate. Bridgeman
assured him that he would not remove Philip unless the law
demanded it. For not reading the *Prayer Book* service, even
though the law requiring this of ministers had not yet come
into force, Roger Puleston withheld Philip's annuity and twice
he was unjustly summoned to appear before the Flint Assizes.
Eventually, in October 1661, Bridgeman dismissed Philip Henry
from his charge, and on the Sunday following he preached his
farewell sermon to the parishioners of Worthenbury. For the
sake of peace he later received some of the arrears due to him
from the Emral estate, but only on condition that he surrendered
all the benefits with which his patron Sir John Puleston had

endowed him, most notably the house specially built for him, which is what the young Puleston was eager to obtain.

It was while Philip Henry was undergoing these severe trials that he married the girl he had fallen in love with some years before. Katharine Matthews was the only child of a well-to-do farmer at Broad Oak, some seven miles east of Worthenbury and within three miles of Whitchurch in Shropshire. On both sides of her family she was of Welsh ancestry. Her father discouraged her at first and friends objected, arguing that although Philip was a scholar and preacher they did not know where he came from. 'True,' replied Katharine, 'but I know where he is going, and I should like to go with him.' Philip finally won the consent of Katharine's father and the marriage took place on 26 April 1660. It proved a most happy relationship despite the difficulties they encountered. Their first child, John, arrived the following year while they were still living in Worthenbury. Matthew was born in October 1662 under a different roof.

2

Early life

Moving house is stressful at the best of times. How much more so for a pregnant mother already nursing a one-year-old son, and a father deprived of the ministry to which he had been called and the parishioners he had grown to love! Unlike many ejected ministers, Philip and Katharine were not destitute. They sought sanctuary in Katharine's family farmstead at Broad Oak. Katharine's parents actually lived a short distance away at her father's home in Bronington, which lay within the Hanmer parish. Relations between Philip Henry and his father-in-law became strained after the birth of their first son, John. Daniel Matthews wanted his grandson to be called Henry Matthews; presumably because he considered him to be the son he never had. There was an embarrassing situation in the church before the child was named and baptized, with Philip insisting that his son's surname should be Henry. His father-in-law took such offence over the issue that from then to the day of his death he never darkened the door of their home. Philip tried his best to regain his friendship, and before Daniel Matthews died there was a softening in his spirit.

Birth

It was at this Broad Oak farmhouse in the most easterly corner of North Wales, close to where the English counties of Cheshire and Shropshire meet, that Matthew Henry was born and brought up. Like his brother John the year before, he arrived earlier than expected and without a midwife's help. He was born at about 3 o'clock on Saturday morning, 18 October 1662, just a fortnight after his parents moved from Worthenbury. Using biblical language, and conscious of the sad situation ecclesiastically, his father wrote in his diary, 'We have no reason to call him Benoni ['son of my sorrow', see Gen. 35:18]—I wish we had not to call him Ichabod' ['no glory', see 1 Sam. 4:21]. The baptism of the newly born infant took place the following day. It was quite normal for those times, if mother and child were well, for the baby to be sealed with the covenant sign in baptism on the first Lord's Day after the birth. Katharine, his mother, had found it comparatively easy to give birth and there were no accompanying complications. The baby was also in good health as noted by his father: 'He hath all his parts & is a comely child for in Thy book all his members were written'. Like other Puritans of Presbyterian persuasion, his father considered the traditional practice of having the new mother 'churched' and of appointing godparents, as the Anglican *Prayer Book* required, to be unnecessary. The suddenness and timing of the birth probably made it easier for the baptism to take place with no unseemly argument in church over the naming of their second son. He was named Matthew in recognition of his mother's maiden name, and possibly with the hope that it would go some way to appease the wrath of grandfather Matthews.

Matthew's father, however, was most displeased at the way his son was baptized. Since the baptism of John the year before, the state's ecclesiastical measures had dramatically changed the local religious scene. Many of Philip Henry's ministerial friends in the area had been ejected from their churches. This was the case with the Presbyterian, George Mainwaring, one of the two ministers belonging to the Malpas parish in Cheshire, near to the Welsh border. He had baptized Philip's first son John while the family was still living in Worthenbury. The Henry family now worshipped on Sundays at the conveniently placed Whitewell chapel, which was but a short walk from Broad Oak. The chapel, though in Wales, came under the oversight of the Malpas parish. With Mainwaring gone on account of his nonconformity it was William Holland, a colleague of Mainwaring but one who conformed under the Act of Uniformity, who carried out the baptism at Whitewell. This clergyman ignored the father's wishes by making the sign of the cross as he baptized the child. This weighed heavily on Philip's mind for some time. He regretted he had not performed the ordinance himself to avoid what he, along with other Puritans, considered to be a superstitious, popish practice. Whatever the consequences, Philip made sure it would not happen again by having Matthew's four sisters baptized privately either by himself or (in the case of Eleanor) by a friend from Oxford.

Health problems

There are few details of Matthew's earliest years. While he was not yet a year old he fell out of bed in the night, but mercifully he was not hurt. A month into his second year they began to wean him off his mother's milk. In those days every childhood sickness was even more life-threatening than it is today and Matthew's parents had a number of anxious moments during his childhood. The measles that resulted in the death of his older brother John shortly before his sixth birthday seems to have placed Matthew's life in the balance too, but he recovered, much to the relief of his parents. When he turned three they suspected that he might have caught smallpox, but it turned out to be a false alarm. They therefore gave grateful thanks to God when Matthew, now their only son and heir, reached the age of seven unscathed.

Matthew's health, however, continued to be a concern to his parents into adulthood. As he neared his tenth birthday they were troubled over his condition; and again the following year he was so unwell that his parents were particularly worried. They committed their son to the Lord and God graciously gave him back to them. Even when Matthew was in his late teens and early twenties, his father's letters to him while he studied in London contain frequent references to his son's health and often urge him, for instance, not to take a Thames boat to see his aunts in case he developed a cold that would lead to more serious ailments.

Home life

The home into which Matthew was born was the very best of Puritan families. His parents had a great love and respect for each other and Philip Henry never forgot the date of their marriage. On their twentieth wedding anniversary Matthew's father wrote: 'We have been so long married and never reconciled; that is, there never was any reason for it'. Together they loved and sought to instruct and discipline in a God-honouring way their son Matthew and his four sisters, Sarah, Katharine, Eleanor and Ann, who were born in quick succession from 1664 to 1668.

Sunday was specially set apart from the rest of the week as God had commanded. Matthew recalls how his father greeted them on the Lord's Day in a way similar to the early Christians: 'The

Lord is risen; he is risen indeed.' Despite his treatment by state and church, Philip Henry dutifully took his family to the Church of England services at Whitewell chapel every Sunday, morning and afternoon, whenever they had a preacher, which was usually twice a month. He would even bring the clergyman home for a meal. Afterward they would sing a psalm. Philip would repeat the morning sermon to all present and pray. The ministry they received in their local church was often less than satisfactory. Several times in his diary, Matthew's father comments adversely on the preaching he heard. On one occasion he speaks of 'two empty, frothy, flashy, unprofitable sermons ... Lord pity preacher and hearers.' For 8 November 1663 he writes: 'Text Romans 5:1, a most full text, a most empty sermon!'

In the evening, after the afternoon service, Philip would preach to his family. When there was no preaching at Whitewell, the family spent the whole day at home and Philip would preach to them. Neighbours hungry for the Word of God would drop in as well. After the First Conventicle Act was passed in May 1664 it became illegal for anyone aged sixteen and over to attend a meeting for worship that was not in accordance with the Anglican *Prayer Book* and where five or more people over and above family members were present. Fines and imprisonment were imposed, the maximum penalty being transportation to the colonies. A Second Conventicle Act came into force in 1670 with more stringent penalties, including heavy fines on preachers or householders who allowed their homes to be used for such worship services.

During these years of oppression and persecution, family worship took on even more significance. In the Henry household, with servants as well as children attending, daily worship was made to be a pleasant experience rather than a chore. It was never long and tedious. Morning and evening,

Matthew's father would begin with a short prayer, the singing of a psalm and the reading of a Bible passage with short practical comments. This was followed by questions to the children on what had been read and expounded, and the time ended with prayer and the benediction. On Thursday evenings, instead of reading, he catechized his children and servants, using the Westminster Assembly's *Shorter Catechism* with proof texts.

Philip Henry taught Matthew and his siblings, while they were still very young, to pray according to the pattern set by their father and encouraged them to meet together on their own to pray and sing psalms, especially on Saturday afternoons. Matthew was given the task of leading these meetings. If he thought his sisters were too short in their prayers, he would gently tell them of all the people and situations they could bring to the Lord in prayer. His sisters acknowledged, much later in life, how they had been greatly encouraged and helped by their brother's remarks and example. On Saturday evenings, they were asked to recall what they had been taught during the week and their father helped them understand what they had found hard to comprehend. He also encouraged them to write down everything they found helpful in what they heard from their father or read in the Bible and other good books. Notebooks were given to each of them for this purpose. No doubt Matthew found these jottings of his father's pithy remarks most useful when he came to write his commentary.

His father also drew up a short form of the baptismal covenant which he taught his children. Every Sunday evening Matthew and each of the girls would, in turn, solemnly repeat it and their father would say 'Amen' after each item. As they grew older he urged them to freely and cheerfully consent to what they repeated by heart and helped them to understand clearly what they were saying.

Conversion

When Matthew and his sisters came to their mid-teens they were encouraged most earnestly and with due preparation to take the ordinance of the Lord's Supper and to be full church members. For these children, Matthew included, this commitment to Christ and his people was no formal accepted practice carried out because it was 'the done thing' at the age of sixteen. There are clear evidences that between the ages of ten and eleven Matthew had become a true believer. It was through a sermon preached by his father on Psalm 51:17 that his heart was melted and he was encouraged 'to enquire after Christ'. At the age of eleven, in true Puritan fashion, Matthew noted several marks preachers had mentioned that gave evidence of being a child of God and questioned himself as to the sincerity of his Christian profession. On his thirteenth birthday he praised God for his mercies toward him, including the blessings that come through Jesus Christ, and added: 'Lord Jesus I bless thee for thy word, for good parents, for good education, that I was taken into covenant betimes in baptism; and, Lord, I give thee thanks, that I am thine, and will be thine'. He was even more eager to hear his father's sermons and was often so moved by them that he went to his room weeping and praying that the impressions made on him by the message would not be lost.

3

Education

Matthew may not have been the most robust of children, but he certainly had an alert mind and was a quick learner. At the age of three he could read the Bible clearly and with a knowledge and appreciation of the text few twice his age were capable of achieving. His father, prevented by law from engaging in the work to which he had been called, was in a better position than most fathers to give attention to his son's early education. Besides teaching Matthew and his daughters to read and write, he encouraged them to memorize the sermons they heard preached and to write them out in full afterwards.

A nasty piece of legislation was introduced in 1665, called the Five Mile Act. It was aimed at breaking the connection between nonconforming ministers and their former parishioners. Those clergymen who refused to swear an oath never to attempt to resist the king or alter the present status quo of church and state, including swearing obedience to the 1662 *Prayer Book*, were forbidden (among other things) to enter within five miles of any place where they had served as a minister. It was an impossible law to police in all its details; and after initial zealous efforts were made to enforce it, in many areas, especially where there was more sympathy for the nonconformists, a blind eye was often turned when it was flouted.

Although Broad Oak was reckoned to be only four miles from the boundary of Worthenbury parish, Matthew's father arranged for the distance to be measured exactly and found that it was just over five miles. To satisfy local enforcement agencies, who went by reputed rather than precise miles, he left home for a time and resided with friends across the border in England. Later, in 1667, he took his wife and children with him and they made their home for about a year in Whitchurch. Philip's idea was not only that he should be seen to be abiding by the law, but also to be closer to the school he wished his son John to attend and to which he intended to send Matthew when he was old enough. With John's death soon after their move and the Five Mile Act losing its bite, Philip took his wife and five-year-old Matthew back to Broad Oak.

Home schooling

Matthew's sister, Sarah, nearly two years younger than him, was taught biblical Hebrew by her father when she was about six or seven, using a grammar book he had devised for the purpose. Although there is no record to prove it, it is highly likely that this was the way Matthew picked up his knowledge of the language. By the time he was six, however, his father provided him with his own personal tutor. His teacher was fifteen-year-old William Turner (1653–1701) from Marbury in Cheshire. He was the first of a number of young scholars that Matthew's father received into his home in order to prepare them for going to university. He entered St. Edmund Hall, Oxford, in 1669. After graduating M.A. in 1675 he entered the Anglican Church and became vicar of Walberton, Sussex. Matthew's father kept up the friendship with Turner throughout his life, corresponding with him often. Other scholars came and went in quick succession, providing a mutually beneficial arrangement: they were helped and instructed prior to entering university and possible ministry, and Matthew was tutored in the elements of Latin and Greek grammar.

It is clear from these associations that Matthew's father was no bigot. He did not cut himself off from those who had conformed, believing that every man must do as his conscience directs. Matthew himself was to display a similar charitable spirit when he grew up. As a result of the state's draconian measures against all dissent, an education at the two English universities was now closed to Nonconformists. Many, especially those with Presbyterian leanings, conformed in order to receive a degree from Oxford or Cambridge, or in order to obtain civil or military positions which the Corporation and Test Acts disallowed, or to be episcopally ordained in order to minister in the state church. While Philip Henry was prepared to help such people, whose motives were honourable, he later became more aware of the spiritual disadvantages of encouraging young men to enter these universities as preparation for gospel ministry. Although the temptation to conform to the state religion for the sake of Matthew's education was strong, he nevertheless held firmly to his principles and provided other means that he believed would be of more benefit to his son's future work.

While his father was in London for a month during the summer of 1671 visiting his aunts, preaching and meeting with ministers and dignitaries, Matthew wrote him a letter in which we not only learn of his progress in his studies but of a spirituality beyond his years. It reads: 'Every day since you went, I have done my lesson, a side of Latin, or Latin verses, and two verses in the Greek Testament. I hope I have done all well, and so I will continue till you come.' On hearing that a relative was suffering some illness, young Matthew added: 'By this providence we may see that sin is the worst of evils, for sickness came with sin. Christ is the chief good; therefore, let us love him. Sin is the worst of evils, therefore, let us hate that with a perfect hatred.' Already we detect in this nine-year-old the kind of style and content that is such a feature of his commentary.

Doolittle's Academy

Before Matthew reached his eighteenth birthday his father arranged for him to be placed in the family and under the tuition of Thomas Doolittle (1631/2–1707) at Islington, which lay outside the northern walls of the city of London. This bold Puritan preacher was born in Kidderminster and was converted under the ministry of the renowned Richard Baxter (1615–1691). He studied at Pembroke Hall, Cambridge, and after Presbyterian ordination, became pastor to the parishioners of St. Alphage, London Wall. With the passing of the Act of Uniformity he chose to be a Nonconformist and opened a boarding school, first at Moorfields and then Bunhill Fields. The plague of 1665 forced him to retreat to Epping. After the great fire he returned to London in 1666. In defiance of the law, he erected preaching places to cater for worshippers, as their church buildings lay in burnt-out ruins. He came to reside in Islington, where his school became an academy for 'university learning.' Edmund Calamy (1671–1732), the historian, was one of his later students. As it was illegal to engage in such activities, Doolittle was forced to move his seat of learning from place to place. It was while he was again residing in Islington from 1680 to 1683, having narrowly escaped arrest while in Wimbledon, that Matthew Henry entered his academy. Richard Baxter was of the opinion that Matthew could not be in a better place than with Doolittle.

His father and a cousin, Robert Bosier, accompanied Matthew

to London in July 1680. Their journey took them via Newport, Shropshire, to Wolverhampton, then through Birmingham to Stratford-on-Avon, Oxford, Wickham, Uxbridge and Chelsea, where they spent an hour with one of his aunts who was unwell, before pressing on to the City of London. It was an eventful experience for a young man from a rural and more isolated part of the country. It took them five whole days, from Monday to Friday, to reach the great city. In a letter to his sisters, Matthew tells of how he watched the judges process to church at the opening of the assizes in Oxford, and how he heard the assize sermon from the text of Hosea 4:1: 'the LORD hath a controversy with the inhabitants of the land'. The pomp and ceremony would have captivated the wide-eyed Matthew; but this was nothing compared with the sights and sounds of London.

They arrived in the city in the evening, and Matthew was amazed at all the coach traffic that passed them before they reached their inn near Aldersgate. The following day, while his father went to Islington, he and his cousin were treated to a sightseeing tour that took in Bedlam and the Monument. This colossal Doric column, erected as a permanent memorial of the Great Fire, had been completed just three years before Matthew first gazed at what was then among the tallest structures in sight. He climbed the 311 steps (Matthew counted 345 steps!), as tourists to London still do today, to view 'the whole city'. After the devastating fire that had consumed or severely damaged thousands of houses, the city's gates and many public buildings and churches, there was much building work going on, including the new St Paul's Cathedral (begun in 1675 and not completed until 1710).

Bedlam, a corruption of Bethlem (a shortened form of Bethlehem, 'house of bread' in Hebrew), is the world's first and oldest institution to specialize in mental illnesses. Its origins arise out of Christian ministry to the poor and homeless in Bishopsgate and it began admitting mentally ill patients in 1357. Eventually it became a royal hospital and from 1557 was controlled by the city of London. It had become by this time a place notorious for the brutal treatment administered to the patients. Five years before Matthew's arrival, Bedlam moved to new buildings at Moorfields, just outside the city boundary. Matthew made no comment to his sisters about what he saw there; but soon after his return to Broad Oak, on his twentieth birthday, among the twenty-six 'Mercies Received' that he wrote out he mentions his gratitude that he had all his faculties and was not impaired by 'frenzies, lunacy, etc.' After probably seeing so many more disabled people in London than he had been used to, he also included such mercies as 'that I was neither born, nor by accident made, blind, or deaf, or dumb, either in whole, or in part ... that I am not lame or crooked, either through original, or providential want, or a defect, or the dislocation of any part, or member.'

On their first Sunday in London they attended morning worship at Mr Doolittle's large meeting place in Monkwell Street. It had several galleries, 'pewed seats' and 'a brave pulpit, a great height above the people'. They heard Doolittle preach from Jeremiah 17:9 after they had sung a psalm and he had prayed. In the afternoon Matthew's father preached from Lamentations 3:22. At five o'clock Matthew and his cousin Robert visited another place of worship in Westminster that was full to overflowing with people. They were treated to 'a most excellent sermon' from a twenty-three-year-old newly ordained preacher on the evil of sin. This young man was John Shower (1657–1715), who later became a celebrated gospel minister in that part of the city known as Old Jewry, the ghetto of medieval London. Shower had only been ordained the year before by five ejected ministers headed by Richard Adams, and was assistant to Vincent Alsop of Tothill Street Westminster until 1683.

On Monday morning they all went to Islington and Matthew viewed the confined dingy place where he and his cousin Robert would be staying, far different from the more spacious accommodation he was accustomed to at Broad Oak. They also met Mrs Doolittle and her daughter. Philip Henry paid for their 'Bed, Bedstead, Bed-clothes' and other similar items, which cost in all £6. 13s. 6d. (worth about £1000 today).

Life-threatening illness

Robert Bosier was older than Matthew and had entered St Edmund Hall, Oxford, for a time before quitting and residing with the Henrys at Broad Oak in order to be better fitted for Christian ministry among the Nonconformists. With Matthew entering Doolittle's Academy, the Henrys were well pleased that cousin Robert would also further his studies in that institution and believed the cousins would be an encouragement and blessing to each other. Things did not turn out as anticipated. No sooner had his father returned home at the beginning of August, having, among other things, bought a few books, than his son became ill with a fever. He recovered for a while but toward the end of the same month his anxious parents were deeply concerned when his condition worsened.

By the beginning of September cousin Robert, who had been reporting to the family the life-threatening condition of their son, himself began to feel unwell, along with others in the house and neighbourhood. Despite the efforts of medical doctors this godly young man, much to the grief and disappointment of relatives and friends, died just after reaching the age of twenty-three on 13 September and was buried in a new graveyard near the Artillery ground. This burial ground is known as Bunhill Fields, opposite what is now Wesley's Chapel, where many famous Nonconformists were interred, including John Bunyan, John Owen and Thomas Goodwin.

Much to the relief of his parents and sisters, Matthew slowly recovered from his near-death experience. He had been in a mind to return home soon after he arrived, and this recent tragic event convinced him that this was the best policy. The tuition may have been outstanding; but the conditions in and around the place he was staying left much to be desired. Though still weak, he travelled home on the Chester coach later that September and his parents were very relieved and thankful to God as they welcomed him back to Broad Oak.

It was no doubt a big disappointment to him, as it was to his father, that he had spent barely two months in Islington under Doolittle; but what little he was taught in such difficult circumstances, together with the studies he resumed under the mentorship of his father, was much appreciated and he felt he had made good progress. In the same list of mercies that he itemized on his twentieth birthday to which we have already referred, Matthew is most thankful for the 'liberal education' he had received and that he had been given 'a capacity for, and been bred up to, the knowledge of the languages, arts, and sciences; and that, through God's blessing on my studies, I have made some progress therein.'

4

Gray's Inn

One of Philip Henry's trusted friends was the godly and learned Roland Hunt (1629–1699) of Boreatton, Shropshire, son of Colonel Thomas Hunt. He married Lady Frances, the daughter of Lord Paget, and was the high sheriff of Shropshire in 1672. Henry acted as pastor to the family, ministering the Lord's Supper to them from time to time. After he left Doolittle's Academy, Matthew was a frequent and welcome visitor to their home. Hunt advised Matthew to study law at one of the London Inns of Court. Many reasons have been offered as to why this course of action was suggested; for it was not in Matthew's mind to enter the legal profession. Perhaps Hunt considered it would be valuable experience, especially as his previous attempt to further his education in the capital had come to a premature end. It was quite common for young men who had no intention of becoming barristers or judges to study there. In the uncertain and difficult times through which they were passing, when rumours of rebellion and plots made king and government nervous and led to a period of sustained persecution of Nonconformists, it might also have seemed a sensible course of action.

Whatever the reason, father and son discussed and approved of the idea, with the result that Matthew returned to London in April 1685, aged twenty-two, to commence his studies in Gray's Inn. Of the four Inns, Gray's rose to prominence during the reign of Elizabeth. Many noblemen and illustrious figures became members including William Juxon (1582–1663), Archbishop of Canterbury, and Francis Bacon (1561–1626). By the time Matthew entered it was experiencing a period of decline: admissions per year fell from over a hundred to an average of fifty-seven.

Matthew's journey to the great city was uneventful. His parents were glad to hear that he had arrived safely and without incident. The first letter he received from his father highlighted the concerns they felt at home for his physical as well as his spiritual well-being. It ended wishing him some of the fresh air of the countryside, perfumed with May blossom, in place of 'your offensive town-smels, against which you have need to arm your self, especially at first til you are us'd to them'.

From the moment he got there Matthew gave himself to study, so that his poor father was concerned that he was over-working. He clearly had loving yet somewhat over-protective parents who were anxious about their son's health and eating habits. Letters from home advised him not to injure his health by fasting or mingling where crowds assembled. They suggested reading in the morning and later in the day to make time to meet people, visit places and acquaint himself with the affairs of the day. In one of his letters his father was worried about Matthew's intention of journeying to Sussex. He hoped there would be a fast coach and that he would be with suitable companions as 'alone I would not have you, by no meanes, to venture in a strange country'.

Although it was May, the weather had been rather wet and that added to his father's unease, as it would make travelling even more treacherous for coach and horse.

Very aware of the temptations in London to become less earnest in spiritual matters and for worldly pleasures to attract the unwary, his father was, above all his other concerns, eager to encourage his son to walk closely with God. 'Be careful, my dear child, in the main matter. Keep yourself always in the love of God let nothing come, however not abide, as a cloud between you and his favour, for in that is *life*.' His mother was as concerned as his father. Here is a piece she wrote in the absence of her husband:

> I write a line or two to you to mind you to keep in with God, as I hope you do, solemn, secret, daily prayer … not forgetting what you have been taught, and the covenant engagements, renewed again and again that you lie under, to walk circumspectly, in your whole conversation; watching against youthful lusts, evil company, sins and snares from the world, and the devil. Your affectionate Mother, K.H.

Such letters kept coming each week while he was at Gray's Inn and Matthew dutifully wrote back immediately with news of his activities. In them all he expressed his own personal piety. How his parents must have been relieved and heartened to receive letters from their son. Here is a typical example:

> The more I see of the world and the various affairs of the children of men in it, the more I see of the vanity of it and the more I would fain have my heart taken off from it, and fixed upon the invisible realities of the other world.

These weekly letters flowed back and forward from Broad Oak to Gray's Inn. In one letter Matthew comments on the speedy way in which letters reached their destination, despite being handled by many strangers, 'in the space of sixty hours'! At the same time, he used the observation to illustrate how much quicker and easier it is to send messages to heaven at all hours.

Matthew was encouraged to meet up with his aunts and uncles and to visit Whitehall to see where his father was born and grew up. Philip Henry's father, Matthew's grandfather, a Welshman from near Swansea, had been a servant to Charles I. Matthew's father had played with the present king, Charles II and his brother, the future James II, when they were children. Matthew was also directed to call on his father's former close colleagues in the ministry, who had been forced into nonconformity by the Act of Uniformity and who had eventually made their way to London, where it was generally easier to minister without too much harassment. They included Edward Lawrence (1623–1695), a Cambridge graduate, who was removed from Baschurch, Shropshire, and then forced to move from Whitchurch by the Conventicle Act and Richard Steele (1629–1692), a graduate of both Cambridge and Oxford, who was ejected from Hanmer parish church near Philip's home and forced to leave the area due to the Five Mile Act.

Severe persecution

Matthew was back home three months later, possibly bringing Ann, one of his father's sisters, with him; at least, that was his father's hope. It was during this period that Philip Henry was taken prisoner together with some Nonconformist ministers from Lancashire, and held at Chester Castle for about three weeks. It was the time of the Duke of Monmouth's rebellion in the West Country and the culmination of various rumours and plots against Charles II and his brother James, who became king in 1685. The authorities were understandably nervous, especially as James had converted to Roman Catholicism. Up to that point, Philip Henry had generally been treated well by the local magistrates. Even the dreaded Judge George Jeffreys respected Philip and would have nothing said against him when, as Chief Justice of Chester, he had sat as judge at the Flint assizes in Mold. Philip was a great friend of Jeffreys' mother, a pious woman who lived at Acton Hall, Wrexham, and he had examined her son George when he was a pupil at Shrewsbury school. But now, as Lord Chief Justice, Jeffreys was in Taunton handing out his grim sentences at the 'bloody assizes' on those caught up in the rebellion, and would go down in history as the 'hanging judge.'

Philip Henry had mentioned Monmouth's invasion in his letter to Matthew in London on 20 June 1685. At that time he wrote of keeping a low profile at home and saying little as he was suspected of having sympathies with the rebellion. It did not help ministers like Philip, who were of Presbyterian persuasion, that there was rebellion in Presbyterian Scotland, led by the Duke of Argyll, and that the fanatical Presbyterian minister, Robert Ferguson, took a leading part in the Monmouth uprising. Matthew wrote to his father while he was confined in Chester Castle, in which he was pleased to know that he was being treated well. Matthew wanted to visit him, but his friends urged against it. The day after his father was released from his imprisonment, Matthew heard him recount God's mercies toward him while confined. He was grateful that he was held for no good reason, for 'it is guilt that makes a prison'; that it meant his security in a dangerous time; that he had good fellowship with fellow prisoners; that he was in health, visited and prayed for by friends; that he was in cheerful spirits and was able to sleep peacefully; and that the magistrates had nothing with which to charge him. This positive way of treating God's severe providences would be later seen in the life of his son Matthew.

Richard Baxter

It was in May of that same troubled year that Richard Baxter, former minister of Kidderminster, was brought to trial before Judge Jeffreys. Since coming to the London area he had been in trouble with the law on many occasions, but this was his worst encounter. Baxter was found guilty of libelling the Church of England and sentenced to pay a large fine and to lie in prison till it was paid, and also bound to good behaviour for seven years. Matthew may well have been present for the trial. What is certain is that he visited his father's old friend in Southwark, accompanied by his close friend, Samuel Lawrence (1661–1712), the nephew of Edward Lawrence. Although Baxter was a prisoner, he found him in a private house near the prison with his own servant and maid. Baxter was reluctant to receive the gift his father had sent by Matthew's hand, and Matthew learned later that his needs were not great. But they had about an hour with the old saint, who enquired after his friends in Shropshire (from which he hailed and where he first ministered). Matthew found the visit very beneficial, for instead of them ministering to Baxter, it was Baxter who was ministering to them, giving the young men much spiritual advice, especially for the difficult times through which they were passing.

Matthew used his time at Gray's Inn to further his knowledge by attending French classes for three months. His father, in giving his consent, wished he had knowledge of the language, so that he could read for himself what was written in a French catechism referred to by the Bishop of St Asaph. His sister Katharine was hoping he would teach her French, but playfully added: 'but I think they say *one* tongue is enough for a woman'! Being in London enabled Matthew to attend all the interesting meetings and disputations that the capital afforded. One he especially enjoyed was a debate concerning the place of faith in justification; whether it was a condition, as Baxter and his followers were maintaining, or an instrument. Baxter's revision of the Reformation teaching on justification became very popular. Though his views were unacceptable to Philip and Matthew Henry, they did not fully appreciate what disastrous results his beliefs would have, especially among dissenting ministers.

Before he left home, Matthew was looking forward to hearing sermons from some of the well-known names in the city, and his father made sure he did not lose this interest. He urged him to hear English as well as Latin sermons, to reflect on what he heard, and to make notes of the headings when he returned to his digs. In his reports home, no reference is made to any dissenting ministers that he heard. During this period when Presbyterians in particular came under suspicion by the government, Matthew only mentions preachers of the state church. They included John Tillotson (1630–1694), a future Archbishop of Canterbury, who was of Presbyterian background but conformed in 1662. Matthew heard him occasionally giving the Tuesday lectures at St. Lawrence Jewry. On Sundays he attended St. Andrew's, Holborn, near Gray's Inn, where the celebrated Dr Stillingfleet (1635–1699) was ministering. He was a noted preacher and sympathetic to reconciliation with Presbyterians. Both Stillingfleet and Tillotson were less Calvinistic and gospel-centred in their messages. Matthew missed this emphasis and called to mind those 'Broad Oak Sabbaths', under his father's ministry.

Future direction

Matthew was back home in June 1686, returning with items he had been asked to purchase. These included some small Bibles, reasonably priced, but much better bound than the ones his father could obtain locally. The concern now in the country was over James II and his pro-French, pro-Roman Catholic policies. They led to him ruling without Parliament from November

1685 until his enforced abdication in December 1688. Matthew continued his studies at Gray's Inn well into the spring of 1687. At this uncertain time for the country his own mind was taken up with the work to which he felt called.

On his departure from Gray's Inn, the future direction of his life was clearly observed in the farewell sermon he preached to his fellow students. It was a clear and most earnest message, suitable to the occasion, based on the latter part of 2 Thessalonians 2:1: 'and by our gathering together unto him'. Mindful of the context in which Paul was urging the believers not to be troubled or shaken by erroneous teachings concerning Christ's second coming, Matthew proceeded to show the pastoral heart of the apostle. He then went on to expound the glorious prospect of this final great gathering at the resurrection of the dead, which is anticipated in conversion when people are gathered from the world through the preached word as well as when they are gathered together in death. He urged his fellow students to make their calling and election sure, asking them whether they had deliberately and sincerely taken God in Christ to be their God and given themselves up to be his. He pressed home the point: 'If not, do it, and do it quickly ... God is ready to covenant with you; why will not you be as ready to covenant with him? Are not the terms sweet, and easy and gracious, and highly reasonable, that if you will be for him, he will be for you? Could they be better?' In closing he showed the comfort that the final gathering brings to Christians. They may now be scattered over the world; but then all would be together with no one missing. He made reference to the present divisions in the church, to the disorders and troubles, to the restraints on assembling together as well as to removal by death or distance; but at the future gathering there would be no disturbances and restrictions and all would be united and together.

5

Preparing for ministry

Matthew felt drawn to the Christian ministry from childhood days. Like many a boy who goes through a phase of wanting to follow in his father's footsteps and of copying what grown-ups do, Matthew had early desires to be a preacher. He enjoyed imitating the different styles of preaching he saw and heard—not in any disrespectful way, but because he wanted to emulate those men who had impressed him as they proclaimed God's word. When still a young child he had always appreciated the company of the many ministers who frequented the home of his parents: he enjoyed meeting those who loved the Lord and prayed together. He would join in the prayers and was eager to repeat sermons to them; and when he read a chapter from the Bible to an assembled gathering in his home he would occasionally seek to comment on the passage in a helpful way. Some were worried that it would lead to pride; but his father encouraged him, believing that he feared God and that God would keep and bless him.

The subjects in which he was schooled helped develop his

intellectual abilities and gave him a good grounding in appreciating the original languages of the biblical text. For instance, in his farewell sermon to the law students, he was not only able to refer to the Greek text but also mentioned that the Hebrew for 'preacher' in the English text of Ecclesiastes 1:1 meant 'a gatherer', and applied it to those who gather lost sheep and bring them to Jesus Christ, who died to save and form them into a special people for himself. Latin and French were also acquired for perusing the important works of the past and engaging in theological discussion. His father had encouraged him to take notes of all the sermons he heard and to write them out in full, a discipline he continued throughout his life. In this way he obtained a considerable grasp of the fundamental truths of the gospel, particularly from his father's sermons, and of the importance of applying the truth to the daily lives of the people. Far from being a distraction, his time studying law was also of help to him in marshalling his material and presenting it in an orderly way.

His godly upbringing

Among the many mercies that he enumerated on reaching the age of twenty, some of which have already been mentioned, he included the blessing of godly parents and sisters, possessing the Scriptures and many good books, and having a heart to delight in studying them. He was grateful that the principles of religion had been instilled into him from his earliest days and that he had the gift of prayer, enabling him to express his mind to God in words of his own; and not only privately but in public on behalf of others present. In addition, he was mindful of the mercy that, as he put it, 'God hath inclined my heart to devote and dedicate myself to him, and to his service, and the service of his church in the work of the ministry, if ever he shall please to use me.'

Thus we can see at the close of his teenage years how settled he was in his desire to be a gospel minister; and those who knew Matthew well could say nothing but good of him and found his company of great spiritual benefit. Nevertheless, given the difficulties of the times for ministering outside the established church, and considering he was still quite young and had not had much exposure to life outside his father's home apart from the brief period he spent at Doolittle's Academy, the advice to further his studies at Gray's Inn had been sensible. In addition to expanding his knowledge, it helped build his character still more, introduced him to a wider company of friends, and made him more aware of new developments and trends in theological and scientific thinking and of the dangers inherent when reason rather than the Bible is given pride of place.

His study at Gray's Inn in no way deflected him from his desire to be a preacher. Though he devoted himself wholeheartedly to the law course he did not enjoy it, and sometimes expressed discouragement that on almost every difficult case there were conflicting opinions even among the best of lawyers. Nevertheless, he persevered in his studies and found much help and inspiration from the company he kept and the preachers he heard.

Pastoral heart

Matthew's concern for the spiritual welfare of others also developed during his time away. He had become friendly with a young man of his age who lived in Nantwich, Cheshire, about fourteen miles from his parents' home at Broad Oak. George Illidge had become a committed Christian at an early age. Having little spiritual support at home, he would make his way to Broad Oak as often as he could on the Lord's Day to come under the ministry of Philip Henry. Matthew had promised to write to him and, prompted by one of his sisters, he wrote a most spiritually helpful letter on 1 March 1686 from Gray's Inn. Illidge was by then a married man and Matthew's letter must have been a great stimulus to him as he sought to live a life worthy of the gospel. Matthew confessed that he had nothing worth writing about his circumstances in London but much to relate concerning what he had been meditating on recently. After mentioning ten items of gospel truth for godly living, he encouraged his friend to talk often about Christ, to be concerned for unconverted neighbours, and to do all he could to help them change. As his biographer J. B. Williams states: 'Were not the reader informed that the writer of the letter was only in his twenty-fourth year, he would almost fancy himself listening to the grave, and matured counsels of hoary, and devout intelligence.'

During the summer of that same year, when Matthew was back at Broad Oak, he was invited through his friend, George Illidge, to preach at Nantwich on several occasions on Sunday evenings. On his final visit a man notorious for his dissolute lifestyle was present and came under great conviction, resulting in a remarkable change in his outward behaviour, although he later fell back after his wife's death some years later. The initial effects of Matthew's preaching were an encouragement to him to continue to believe that his decision to enter the Christian ministry was the right one. But it also cautioned him not to be too impressed by sudden outward changes in a person's life and to be more aware of the deceitfulness of the human heart.

Call

That same summer he was invited to preach to friends in various houses in Chester on a number of evenings and was so well received that they were keen for him to become their pastor. At that time there were still grave restrictions on Nonconformist gatherings for worship; but at the end of 1686, when there were rumours that the government was about to relax restrictions, several people from Chester came to Broad Oak to urge Matthew to take on the oversight of their congregation.

After consulting his father, he was willing to consider this request, provided that one of the revered Chester ministers, old Mr Harvey, gave his consent, and that they allowed him to complete his law studies. The deputation gladly agreed to these terms and returned to Chester hopeful of a successful outcome. Matthew's mother, Katharine, was overjoyed at the thought of her son ministering in Chester and had, in the words of her husband, presented some 'weighty' reasons for accepting the call on the terms proposed.

Meanwhile, back in London there were Nonconformists who were informed that Matthew was settled in his mind concerning gospel ministry, and he was invited to take up a position in the capital. However, he respectfully declined the offer, believing that he was more needed in the country than in and around the great city. Numerous letters from the congregation at Chester urging him to be their pastor as soon as possible convinced him of the rightness of this appointment; and on leaving Gray's Inn he prepared himself for ordination with the utmost seriousness.

He obtained the advice of two men well respected by his father, the Rev. Francis Tallents (1619–1708), who was ejected from St. Mary's church, Shrewsbury, in 1662 and became the Presbyterian Nonconformist minister in the town from 1673 to 1708, and his assistant from 1700, the Welsh-speaking James Owen (d. 1706), who kept an academy at Oswestry from around 1690 before moving to Shrewsbury. Both men preached at Philip Henry's funeral.

Ordination

Before his ordination Matthew sketched out a sermon on 1 Timothy 4:15 in which he set out the nature and work of pastoral ministry and what it is for a man to give himself 'wholly to them.' He also composed a statement entitled 'Serious Self examination before Ordination' which indicated the seriousness with which he undertook this holy calling. It reveals his motives in taking up the work and the principles by which he sought to operate. He asked himself six fundamental questions. The first related to his Christian profession, whether he had seen himself as lost and ruined for ever without Christ; whether he had been deeply humbled and broken on account of his sinful nature and actions; whether he had trusted Christ as his Saviour and whether Christ was more than everything to him; whether he had a hatred of every sin both in himself as well as in others and a longing to be rid of it; whether he had a real love for holiness, delighting in it wherever he saw it, including God's word, God's day and God's people, and longing to be made perfect in holiness. A second question involved an examination of what he had done that was not profitable to his spiritual health, so that he might repent and seek forgiveness and cleansing in the blood of Christ. He then questioned himself concerning his aims and motives for entering the Christian ministry: that it was not, for instance, to enrich himself or to gain a name for himself; and he indicated the great desires of his heart in undertaking the work. Finally he mentioned the resolutions he had for his future ministry, which included having nothing to do with the unfruitful works of darkness, striving to be the very best Christian possible and by the grace of God to perform his ordination vows.

Among the people he consulted concerning his ordination, one person he greatly respected suggested that he should consider being episcopally ordained but without the declarations and oaths to which many of the Puritans objected. He considered the idea very seriously and the pros and cons were weighed up carefully, as we observe from what Matthew wrote down on 28 April 1687. It was a question not of whether it was lawful, for a bishop was viewed as a presbyter in Presbyterian eyes, but whether it was advisable. On the positive side it was advisable because that was the law of the land and all other ordinations were not valid in the eyes of church and state. Presbyterians also agreed that episcopal ordination was valid and if there ever came a time when the Act of Uniformity was abolished, episcopal ordination would perhaps qualify a man for service in the church whereas Presbyterian ordination may not qualify him.

Weighted against these considerations was the powerful argument that it would be tacitly accepting the power of bishops to ordain, a power they had unlawfully usurped. It would also mean being ordained first as a deacon before becoming a presbyter/priest. One who was called to be a gospel minister would find it difficult to claim that he had been moved by the Spirit to take on the role of a deacon, which in scriptural terms involved being set aside to serve tables. After examining all the arguments he came to the conclusion that ordination by presbyters was the most scriptural practice, and that Jesus Christ never meant any of his ministers to become priests other than in the way that is true of all believers or that they must first become deacons.

Matthew always consulted his father before making any final decisions, and the reply he received confirmed his own deliberations. Philip Henry had himself thought long and hard over episcopal ordination and had been in a number of discussions with the bishop of St Asaph over the subject. With this matter settled, without further delay Matthew applied for ordination to the leading Presbyterian ministers in London, ones whom he knew best. So it was on 9 May 1687, after an oral examination and the submission of his thesis in Latin on the subject of 'Are men justified by faith without the works of the law?', and after a full confession of his faith made under ten headings, 'he was solemnly but privately ordained "by imposition of hands, with fasting and prayer"'.

The severe restrictions on Nonconformists were still in place, which accounts for the private meeting. It is also the reason why he did not receive the usual certificate. Those who ordained him, some of whom were 'very aged, and very cautious', signed a brief testimonial which read: 'We, whose names are subscribed, are well assured that Mr Matthew Henry is an ordained minister of the gospel'. The names of the ministers included James Owen of Oswestry and Francis Tallents from Shrewsbury, William Wickens (1614–1699), who kept an academy at Newington Green, Nathaniel Vincent (c. 1639–1697), a fine scholar who was imprisoned on numerous occasions for unauthorized preaching, Edward Lawrence and Richard Steele. It must have been a particularly poignant moment for the last-named minister, as he had officiated thirty years earlier at the ordination of Matthew's father.

Later, when Nonconformists were by law tolerated, Matthew applied for and received a fuller statement from the two surviving members of the ordaining party. It was drawn up by Francis Tallents and signed by him and James Owen on 17 December 1702. It read:

> We, whose names are subscribed, being two of those six who subscribed a certificate concerning the ordination of Mr. Matthew Henry, May 9, 1687, do hereby certify that the said certificate was drawn up so short and general, because of the difficulty of the times; but the true intent and meaning of it

was, that the said Mr. Matthew Henry, after due examination and exercises performed with their approbation did, upon the said 9th of May, 1687, at London, make a full confession of his faith, and solemn dedication of himself to the service of Christ in the work of the ministry, and was thereupon, by imposition of hands, with fasting and prayer ordained, and set apart to the work and office of a gospel minister, by those whose names are subscribed with their own hands to the said certificate.

Before the end of May 1687 Matthew was back with his parents. His sister Sarah, the newly married Mrs Savage and now living near Nantwich, came to Broad Oak to see her brother. She wrote in her diary of 'dear brother safe come home'. The following day, 29 May, being Sunday, they all dutifully worshipped at the Church of England Whitewell chapel; but at night family and friends gathered at Broad Oak to hear Matthew preach 'concerning sparing mercy'. Just two days were then left for him at home before commencing his work as a gospel preacher in Chester at the beginning of June.

6

Chester

In some respects Chester has changed little since the seventeenth century, with its Roman walls and medieval cathedral. The unique medieval Rows of first floor covered walkways, with shop frontages directly above ground level shops and offices that line the main streets of Watergate, Northgate, Eastgate and Upper Bridge Street, still excite visitors today. In the 1680s the city corporation began to take more interest in the city's sanitary conditions, drawing up detailed arrangements for disposing of rubbish and cleaning the Rows and main streets.

Chester was not only a well-known trading centre, but also an important stopping point for travellers between England and Ireland. When Matthew moved to the city in 1687 there were 682 guest beds and stabling for 871 horses, far exceeding any other place in the North West. The significance of the city's standing in the region was also emphasized by the regular stagecoach service to London, begun in 1657, equivalent to a direct high-speed rail link to the capital today. It was a facility that Matthew had often used during his stay as a student in the metropolis. After the

Restoration Chester became a notable social centre for the gentry of the surrounding area and many well-to-do families resided there. The affluence of the seventeenth century city can be seen today in the beautiful black and white properties that were built in the 1600s. Another sign of its prosperity was the number of freemasons who lived there, so that by 1725 the city could boast of three separate lodges.

Presbyterians

There were about 1700 households by the time Matthew came to Chester. Among the inhabitants there was a considerable minority of Dissenters, or Nonconformists as they came to be called. There had been some Independents there prior to the Restoration, but the Act of Uniformity forced many of a Presbyterian persuasion into the company of the Dissenters. Five of the city's ministers had Presbyterian leanings and were ejected in 1662. When the Declaration of Indulgence was promulgated in 1672, a number of meetings were licensed in the city; so that by the end of the year there were complaints that the Nonconformist congregations had grown so much that the city's parish churches were emptying.

Arguably the most important group of Presbyterians were those meeting in White Friars, in the house of Anthony Henthorn, a sugar merchant, where William Cook (who had been ejected from St. Michael's), ministered from 1672. Two other main meeting places existed in 1682: one where Ralph Hall, an ejected minister from Staffordshire, was granted permission to teach; and the other in the house of Hugh Harvey with John Harvey, a former rector of Wallasey, ministering. When renewed persecution broke out in 1682 Hall and Cook ceased to preach (both died in 1684), while Harvey continued to minister secretly, assisted by visiting preachers.

The meeting-place

Matthew Henry's first preaching engagements in Chester had included the house of Anthony Henthorn. Providentially, there was an easing of restrictions through James II's proclamation of the Declaration of Indulgence on 4 April 1687 that suspended, without parliamentary approval, the penal laws enforcing conformity to the state church and allowing people, whether Protestant or Roman Catholic, to worship in their homes or chapels. It enabled Henthorn's underground house church to function legally and for Matthew to be invited without state interference to be their pastor. Pending his arrival, the church had obtained the services of another young man of similar age to Matthew, William Tong (1662–1727), who became Matthew Henry's first biographer. He was later to exercise an influential ministry in London and became a staunch defender of the Trinity at a time when it was being seriously undermined. In the three months he was in Chester, from March to May, Tong's ministry was so successful that the congregation outgrew the spacious room in Henthorn's house, making it necessary for him to open up an adjoining stable that he owned to accommodate the increasing numbers. The members contributed to the cost of making it suitable as a meeting place. At the end of May 1687 Tong moved for a short time to Wrexham to assist Mr John Evans (1628–1700) and his sizeable congregation.

It was on 1 June 1687 that a deputation from Chester escorted Matthew Henry to Henthorn's home. But before he felt able to begin his ministry in Chester, Matthew was determined to visit the aged Mr Harvey. He was eager to hear from Harvey's own lips that he was happy for the newly ordained young preacher to minister in the city. Matthew was aware that people were drawn to the ministry at Henthorn's place rather than to Harvey's preaching despite his faithful work and the hardships endured for the gospel's sake. Having a father who had likewise suffered for his religious principles and who knew Harvey well, Matthew was more sensitive to the feelings of this elderly and increasingly feeble servant of Christ. The venerable preacher satisfied Matthew of his good will toward him and was especially heartened to hear him state that there was work enough for both of them. He therefore commenced his ministry by preaching the Thursday lecture on the text 'For I determined not to know any thing among you, save Jesus Christ, and him crucified' (1 Corinthians 2:2).

About a month later Matthew suggested to Harvey that their congregations should merge. Matthew was willing to offer himself as assistant to the older minister. Failing that, Matthew hoped that the two congregations might join together for the monthly Lord's Supper—they were, after all, worshipping within a stone's throw of one another. In the event, Harvey would not entertain any of Matthew's ideas for closer cooperation. When the Toleration Act of 1689 was passed, giving liberty of worship to Dissenters, he and Harvey obtained licences for their meeting places and Matthew held a Thanksgiving day, preaching from Hosea 2:4.

Congregation

It had been the practice for the congregation to assemble for their own services at times other than those appointed at the cathedral and parish churches for public worship. They actually appreciated the ministry of Laurence Fogg (1623–1718), inducted prebendary of Chester cathedral in 1673, later becoming dean, and both Philip and Matthew thought highly of his preaching despite the unkind things he said about Nonconformists. His father was Robert Fogg, the minister of Bangor-is-y-coed, who was a friend of Philip Henry and among the ejected ministers of Wales. At first the congregation continued to meet at noon and then again in the evening. When insensitive Laurence Fogg informed Edward Gregg that their gatherings were 'schismatical at any time', the congregation decided, for convenience, to move the time of their morning worship to coincide with the Anglican services, especially as the king had granted freedom of worship. The revised meeting times were also adopted by Harvey's congregation in Bridge Street.

Edward Gregg (*c.* 1621–1689) was an Oxford graduate and of Middle Temple and one of the founding members of the church, whom Matthew's father greatly esteemed for his godliness and meekness of spirit. Other influential people who became great friends of Matthew Henry in Chester were wealthy merchants like Giles Vanbrugh and George Mainwaring. Vanbrugh (1631–1689) was the father of Sir John, who became a dramatist and architect, best known as the designer of Castle Howard and Blenheim Palace. When Matthew began his ministry this same son, a staunch young Whig, was already working undercover to overthrow James II and place William of Orange on the throne. Sadly, he had no desire to follow in the godly ways of his parents. Alderman George Mainwaring (1642–1695) had been mayor of the city and a supporter of the Duke of Monmouth. For a short time in 1689 he represented Chester in Parliament. Barrister George Booth (1635–1719) and John Hunt, a younger brother of Rowland Hunt of Boreatton, as well as Anthony Henthorn, were also of like mind to Matthew and faithful members of the congregation.

Marriage

All Matthew's sisters were married by 1689. Apart from Sarah, the eldest, who married John Savage of Wrenbury Wood near Nantwich, they also came under his ministry as their husbands lived in Chester. Katharine married Dr John Tylston of Trinity College, Oxford, a physician; Eleanor married Samuel Radford, a tradesman; and Ann married John Hulton. As for himself, Matthew lost no time, on his arrival in Chester, in obtaining a suitable wife. On 19 July 1687, just over a month after his arrival, he married Katharine, the only daughter of Samuel Hardware of Bromborough on the Wirral, Cheshire. They had got to know each other through the Hardware's son, John, who married a daughter of the Hunts of Boreatton, close friends of the Henrys. Katharine's parents were committed Christians. While her father and brother were happy to see her married to Matthew, her mother had some reservations. She was naturally very protective of her only daughter and wanted to see her settled comfortably. Several gentlemen of means had made offers that had been refused. She was aware that Nonconformist ministers were despised by many and the liberties they presently enjoyed were precarious. Outweighing all these scruples, however, was her high regard for Matthew, whom she had come to value as a minister and friend of the family, and so she quickly relented.

Philip Henry composed a poem to the newly weds that included the following lines of advice:

> Love one another, pray oft together, and see,
> You never both together angry be.
> If one speak fire, t'other with water come,
> Is one provok'd? be t'other soft or dumb.
> Walk low, but aim high, spotless be your life,
> You are a minister, and a minister's wife.
> Therefore as beacons, set upon a hill,
> To angels and to men a spectacle.

After the wedding Matthew Henry and his wife Katharine lived with Mr Gregg for the first few months before taking up residence near to Henthorn's meeting place at White Friars. Mr and Mrs Hardware moved specially to Chester to be near their daughter and son-in-law. Any lingering doubts that her mother may have nursed concerning the rightness of the marriage were soon removed. She had first-hand experience of the godliness and kindness of her son-in-law and both she and her husband appreciated Matthew's biblical preaching and his prayers. Mrs Hardware had the grace to admit that her initial objections had more to do with covetousness and pride than anything of substance.

All the family hopes for a long and happy marriage were soon dashed. Matthew's wife developed smallpox during the late stages of pregnancy and died aged twenty-five soon after giving birth to their first child on Thursday 14 February 1689. Matthew's sister Sarah was quickly on the scene to comfort her brother and Mr Tong, now the Presbyterian-ordained minister at Knutsford in Cheshire, also ministered to the grieving family. Mrs Hardware, according to reports, seems to have borne the sadness with greater composure than her son-in-law and was able to comfort him as well as herself with the words, 'God, who knew how long my child had to live, brought her into Mr. Henry's family to prepare her for heaven.' For Matthew, when he could control his tears, his first words were, 'I know nothing that could support me under such a loss as this, but the good hope that she is gone to heaven, and that, in a little time, I shall follow her thither.'

The funeral took place on Saturday evening at Trinity Church, followed by a sermon at Matthew's meeting-place when Edward Lawrence, who had assisted at Matthew's ordination, preached from Philippians 1:21: 'To die is gain.' It was a great comfort that his first child was spared, and grandfather Philip Henry baptized the infant girl publicly. She was named Katharine after her mother, according to her father's wishes. The large congregation that had assembled for the event was moved to tears by the father's emotional words of dedication:

Although my house be not now so with God, yet he hath made with me an everlasting covenant, ordered in all things and sure, and this is all my salvation, and all my desire, although he make me not to grow; and, according to the tenor of this covenant, I offer up this my child to the Great God, a plant out of a dry ground, desiring it may be implanted into Christ.

7

Joys and sorrows

Matthew maintained a close relationship with his in-laws, who were very kind and thoughtful. Despite his great loss he was enabled to carry on with his ministerial duties without interruption. Mrs Hardware was particularly understanding and made it her business not only to advise him to find a new partner but to recommend one of her own relatives, Mary, the daughter of Robert Warburton of Hefferstone Grange, Cheshire. Her grandfather had been Chief Justice of Chester earlier in the century and chose as his motto which he displayed in every room of his house, 'Christ is the Christian's all'. The home where Mary lived became a safe sanctuary for ministers forced into Nonconformity.

The marriage between Matthew and Mary took place on 8 July 1690 with both sides of the family present. After staying a few days with the Warburtons, Philip and Katharine Henry accompanied the happy couple to Chester, pleased that their son had a most suitable wife once more. The Hardwares were also

very satisfied with the outcome and so, with no further need to
reside in Chester, they returned to their estate in Bromborough.

Diary

Later that year Matthew began to keep a diary which he was able
to continue regularly almost to the end of his life. His first entry
on 9 November 1690 reads:

> This day I concluded my subject of redeeming time from
> Eph.v.16; and, among other things, directed as very useful, to
> keep a short account every night how the day has been spent.
> This will discover what are the thieves of our time, and will
> show us what progress we make in holiness; and now, why
> should not I make the experiment?

At the time when Mary gave birth to a daughter Elizabeth,
12 April 1691, Matthew decided to make a will and added this
memorandum that is a reminder of his biblical perspective on
life:

> I have now set my house in order; and, to the best of my
> apprehension, I have ordered it justly, as becomes my
> obligations of that kind. I have been deliberately weighing
> the case of a 'departure' hence; the things that invite my stay
> here are far from outweighing those that press my departure.
> Through grace, I can say, 'I desire to depart, and to be with
> Christ, which is far better.'

Tragedy struck the Henry home when their one-year old
daughter Elizabeth died after developing whooping cough and
a fever. She had been baptized in the earliest days of her life by
her grandfather, Philip Henry, and had begun to walk, talk and
observe things. Her parents were naturally very proud of her and
she brought them great delight. Just three days before she left this
life Matthew penned these words:

The child has had an ill night; she is very weak, and in all appearance worse; but I am much comforted from her baptism. I desire to leave her in the arms of Him who gave her to me. The will of the Lord be done. I have said, if the Lord will spare her, I will endeavour to bring her up for him. I am now sitting by her, thinking of the mischievous nature of original sin, by which death reigns over poor infants.

On the day she died, 19 July 1692, he wrote these touching words that, far from driving him away from God, encouraged him to trust that she was in safe keeping:

In the morning I had the child in my arms, endeavouring solemnly to give her up to God, and to bring my heart to his will; and presently there seemed some reviving. But while I was writing this, I was suddenly called out of my closet. I went for the doctor, and brought him with me; but, as soon as we came in, the sweet babe quietly departed between the mother's arms and mine, without any struggle, for nature was spent by its long illness; and now my house is a house of mourning.

Covenant children

The death of Elizabeth came five years to the day after Matthew had married his first wife, Katharine, and that caused him to reflect more on his present loss. He called to mind the fondness he had for his little daughter and added:

I had set my affection much upon her. I am afraid too much; God is wise, and righteous, and faithful. Even this also is not only consistent with, but flowing from covenant love … Lord wean me from this world by it. Blessed be God for the covenant of grace with me and mine; it is well ordered in all things, and sure. O that I could learn now to comfort others, with the same comforts with which I trust, I am comforted of God! …

My dear wife is much distressed. The Lord sustain her. I would
endeavour to comfort her. We are now preparing for a decent
interment of my poor babe. Many friends come to see us. I am
much refreshed with 2 Kings iv.26.

He spoke of the burial as 'a sad day's work'; but he had his good
friend Mr Lawrence, who had spoken at his first wife's funeral,
to preach a very suitable sermon for the occasion on the text
of Psalm 39:9: 'I was dumb, I opened not my mouth; because
thou didst it'. Matthew's closing words concerning the funeral
are most moving: 'There is now a pretty little garment laid up in
the wardrobe of the grave to be worn again at the resurrection.
Blessed be God for the hope of this.'

Grief turned to joy the following April when they had another
daughter, whom they named Mary. Grandfather Philip was
called again to baptize her and he preached a helpful sermon
from Genesis 33:5, where Esau asked his brother concerning
those with him and Jacob replied that they were 'the children
which God hath graciously given thy servant'. Philip Henry
emphasized that children are the gifts of God and that children
of the covenant are his *gracious* gifts.

This little joy was short-lived; for within three weeks of her
birth she was suddenly taken ill and died. With his father's
sermon still ringing in his ears Matthew wrote: 'The Lord is
righteous: he takes and gives, and gives, and takes again. I desire
to submit: but, O Lord, shew me wherefore thou contendest with
me'. Every severe providence was seen as a means of disciplining
God's people. The words of Job (10:2) when he had lost his
children and all his possessions must have been at the back of
his mind, and it was from Job 38 that Matthew preached to his
morning congregation two days after the sad event. His sister
Sarah was present and heard him ask, 'Was it fit that Job should

quarrel with God as to his particular providences to him, when he was so unacquainted with the methods of his providence in general?'

Today, it would be unthinkable for a pastor to be conducting services when his own child had died; but Matthew not only ministered at the morning meeting but at the evening one as well, preaching from Romans 5:14: 'Nevertheless death reigned from Adam to Moses, even over them that had not sinned after the similitude of Adam's transgression, who is the figure of him that was to come'. His sister Sarah, having had much experience from early years at writing out sermons, gives us a summary of what her brother said. Matthew illustrated the dominion of death in its effects on infants, who, though not guilty of actual sin, were still the subjects of this rule. He then went on to address those who were, or had been, called to lose their little ones, and it clearly reveals that what he was applying to others he was preaching to himself.

Resign, and give up your dying children to God. They cannot do it. You must do it for them. Father, into thy hands I commit my child's spirit. They are his by right: and his by your consent. You should restore them when he calls for them, and do it freely. I know it is hard, but it must be done. Let their death bring your sin to remembrance. Did you not sin in an inordinate desire of children? Perhaps in discontent, or poverty, you have thought them too many. It may be you were over fond of them, or too indulgent. My pride, my passion, my covetousness—these slew my child. Learn to bear it patiently. Do not murmur. If I am bereaved of my children, said the patriarch, I am bereaved; not I am undone. The Shunamite said, It is well—for all is well that God doth. If a sparrow doth not fall without the will of God, then a child doth not. Comfort yourselves at such a time in God's covenant with you, and your seed. Fetch your comforts from the Lord Jesus who was dead, and is alive, and lives for evermore.

He closed by urging his congregation to consider where children are taken from and what they are taken to. 'They are not born in vain, if they help to people the new Jerusalem.'

That same Sunday evening baby Mary was buried in a grave in Trinity Church where the remains of her little sister Elizabeth lay. Matthew wrote: 'The Lord prepare *me* for that cold, and silent grave.'

Before the year 1693 was out Matthew heard of the death of his former mother-in-law, Mrs Hardware. He had ministered to her in her declining days, moved at the sight of a woman that had been so full of life and vigour hardly able to speak. He preached at her funeral on Proverbs 14:32: 'The righteous hath hope in his death.'

At the end of that distressing year in the Henry household, Matthew made the following comment in his diary. While it gives expression to his sorrow and spiritual concerns, it is also full of thankfulness to God and gospel hope.

I have received many mercies the year that is past. I have been brought low, and helped. My dear wife is spared. I am yet in the land of the living, though many have been taken away. But how little have I done for God! What will become of me I know not. I find little growth. If any thing hath at any time affected me this year it hath been some sweet desires of the glory which is to be revealed. I have often thought of it as that which would help me in my present duty.

Philip Henry

The years to the end of the century brought their fair share of joys and sorrows to Matthew and Mary's lives. A third daughter, Esther, was born in September 1694, their first to survive into adulthood. Another daughter, Ann, was born in 1697, but she died of measles complications the following year when an outbreak occurred in Chester. Matthew Henry noted that although many children had the disease at the same time, including their four-year-old daughter Esther, 'yet his was the only one, to his knowledge, that died'. On the day of the burial he wrote: 'I am "in deaths often". Lord teach me how to "die daily". I endeavoured, when the child was put into the grace, to act faith upon the doctrine of the resurrection, believing in Him who quickeneth the dead.'

Prior to this unhappy event, Mary lost her father in April 1696 after a long illness. While his passing brought its pain to the family, they knew that death for him was gain. Matthew's father wrote to him on hearing of Mr Warburton's death, 'Your fathers, where are they? One gone, and the other going, but you have a good Father in heaven, that lives for ever'. Little did either of them think that just two months later he would be taken suddenly.

Philip Henry, now aged sixty-five, had preached on the Lord's Day in his usual lively fashion and had given notice of the public fast day that had been decreed for the following Friday, 26 June, urging the people to come in a right frame of mind to the services arranged for that solemn occasion. On Tuesday 23 June, after a better night's rest than he had known for some time, he conducted family worship as usual, although somewhat shorter in prayer than was his custom, and then retired to his room. He was found some time later writhing in pain on his bed. It was a couple of hours later that he allowed a message to be sent to Chester to call for his son and for a doctor. Matthew had thought at first to wait until the following morning to make the journey to Broad Oak, as it was late in the day and very wet. However, he thought better of it and at about eight o'clock in the evening he arrived with his brother-in-law, Dr Tylston. Despite being in great discomfort, his father greeted him with the words, 'O son, you are welcome to a dying father; I am now ready to be offered, and the time of my departure is at hand'. He spoke of being on fire, but thanked God that it was not the fire of hell. When some of his near neighbours came to see him he had the presence of mind, despite his discomfort, to urge them to seek Christ while they were in health.

Realizing he was sinking fast, he had a few moments with his dear wife, thanking her for all her love and tender care, leaving a blessing for his children, their spouses and their little ones. To his son who sat under his head he said, 'Son, the Lord bless you and grant that you may do worthily in your generation, and be more serviceable to the church of God than I have been', a wish that God graciously granted. Matthew's last words to his father were, 'Oh, Sir, pray for me that I may but tread in your steps', to which the reply came 'Yea, follow peace and holiness, and let them say what they will'. He would have said more but strength failed. Almost to his last breath he was either praying or quoting Scripture. With his wife holding his hand as he sat up in bed and Matthew supporting his back with a pillow he was not able to finish that victorious Bible verse, 'O death, where is thy-' and moments later breathed his last.

Matthew felt this loss greatly as father and son were very close. His immediate response included these words: 'And now, what is this that God hath done to us? The thing itself, and the suddenness of it, are very affecting ... The Lord calls my sins to remembrance this day, that I have not profited by him while he was with us as I should have done.' In conducting the family worship at Broad Oak later that morning he spoke of it as a 'very melancholy' occasion: 'the place was *Allon Baccuth*, the oak of weeping'. His sister Sarah had her children with her and Matthew records how they 'were greatly affected'. In concluding his diary entry concerning his father's death, using a number of biblical allusions, he wrote, 'among the neighbours was heard nothing but lamentation and mourning; my dear mother cast down, but not in despair. I, for my part, am full of confusion, and like a man astonished'.

The burial did not take place until Saturday, the public fast on Friday taking precedence over everything else. Matthew was prevented from observing the fast with his own congregation in Chester, feeling it his duty to stay at Broad Oak and preach to those whose minister had been removed from them in this sudden way. He called to mind his father's words that 'weeping must not hinder sowing' and he tells how in the course of the day he reminded the people that in the past they 'had kept too many fasts with dry eyes under melting ordinances, but God had caused us to keep this with wet eyes, under a melting providence'. He preached from 2 Kings 13:20: 'Elisha died ... And the bands of the Moabites invaded the land'.

Matthew did not return to Chester until the following Wednesday, when he preached the lecture from the appropriate text of 2 Peter 1:13–14: 'Yea, I think it meet, as long as I am in this tabernacle, to stir you up by putting you in remembrance; knowing that shortly I must put off this my tabernacle, even as our Lord Jesus hath shewed me'. He wrote in his diary: 'O that it might be preached to my own heart, and written there; that ... I may double my diligence'. As he reflects further on his father's death his godly attitude is everywhere evident. He mentions five items. First he praises God that he had such a father, whose life and lip commended the gospel; that he had had him for so long, and that he had not died when he was a child. He regrets that he had not profited more from his father's example of godliness and desires that the remembrance of him will produce greater influences for good upon him. Recognizing how many friends and family had been removed from him in such a short period of time, he prays that God would prepare him for his own hour of death. Aware of his father's good reputation, he saw it as an encouragement for him to be faithful and useful. Finally, he adds: 'This should bring me nearer to God, and make me live more upon him, who is the fountain of living waters. My dear father was a counsellor to me, but Christ is the wonderful Counsellor. He was an intercessor for me, but Christ is an Intercessor that lives for ever, and is therefore able to save to the uttermost.'

When the next celebration of the Lord's Supper came round he used the occasion once more to draw parallels with the death of his father. 'I desire ... to take the Spirit of God to be my reprover, teacher, and counsellor. I was often refreshed in visiting my father, and conversing with him, I would by the grace of God have more fellowship with the Father, and with his Son Jesus Christ, whom I may be free with.' He also vowed by God's grace to be more like his father in those graces for which he was so well liked by others, to be less hasty and to 'learn to be of a cool, mild spirit.'

At the end of that eventful year he recalled how he had preached at the beginning of it from Proverbs 27:1: 'Boast not thyself of to morrow, for thou knowest not what a day may bring forth.' He wrote in his diary: 'My fathers, where are they? And where am I? Hasting after them. I have lost much time this year; but if, through grace, I have got any good, it is a greater indifferency to the things of this world. The Lord increase it.'

More sorrows

The seventeenth century was not over before more sadness and loss came to the Henry family. Three of his sisters, who were among his congregation in Chester, all became seriously ill during the summer of 1697. Katharine, who was married to Dr John Tylston, the Chester physician, recovered; but Eleanor, who had married Samuel Radford, died at the beginning of August; and Ann, who was married to John Hulton, passed away on 6 September aged twenty-eight. 'I find it hard to submit', Matthew wrote in his diary, but continued: 'Let the grace of Christ be sufficient for me. I have said it, and I do not unsay it—Lord, thy will be done.' In a letter to his sister Sarah after Ann's death, he wrote expressing how he had not only lost a sister but a true friend, one of his 'helpers in Christ Jesus', and, again using biblical language, one who was to him 'as my own soul'. Sarah herself later spoke of her as excelling most Christians in piety.

This was not all, for in 1699 his sister Katharine's husband, Dr Tylston, died aged thirty-five. Even more tragically and suddenly, Samuel Radford died just two years after his wife Eleanor, Matthew's sister. They had three daughters and a son who were now bereft of a father as well as a mother. Matthew and his wife legally adopted them into their own family, and the children were later to acknowledge with gratitude the care they all received in the Henry home. In all these distressing experiences there is no hint of complaint against God; rather, Matthew Henry used these hard providences to humble himself before God, to confess his sins and to pray that God would grant spiritual blessings to him and others. On the last day of the year, he asked for God's help in choosing the right subjects for sermons, to be kept from error and that he might be an instrument to win souls to Christ and to build them up. With much feeling and fervour he also prayed for those families who had lost the head of the household ('the beheaded families'), the widows and the fatherless.

8

Changing times

Matthew Henry lived at a time when there was an upsurge in scientific enquiry, much encouraged by Protestant and Puritan belief that humans have a responsibility under God to manage and use the resources of the earth wisely. Arising from such well-intentioned thinking about God's created world, the Royal Society was established in the year of Matthew's birth, the same year that the chemist and physicist, Robert Boyle (1627–1691), published his findings on gases (known as 'Boyle's Law'). While Boyle and others like him worked within the context of God's revealed Word, there were other thinkers and scientists, like John Locke (1632–1704), whose works questioned biblical beliefs. It was becoming fashionable by the turn of the century for those clergymen and college students who had imbibed their ideas to jettison traditional Christian teaching.

In view of these developments one can understand Matthew's concern for the spiritual state of church and country as the new century began. His prayers on the final day of 1701 witness to his deep disquiet:

> The low condition of the church of God ought to be greatly lamented; the protestant interest small, very small; a decay of piety; attempts for reformation ineffectual. Help, Lord!

The new century did bring its own joys and encouragements to the Henry household. Matthew's one and only son, Philip, was born in May 1700, with four more daughters joining the family in the following ten years, all of whom survived infancy. Later, to the grief of the family, Philip despised his godly background, even distancing himself from his illustrious grandfather by adopting his mother's maiden name of Warburton; and it was as Henry Warburton that he represented Chester in Parliament for the Tories in 1747. He also had his grandfather's old meeting-place at Broad Oak pulled down. In view of what became of him, his aunt Sarah's prayers and thoughts at his birth become particularly striking.

> The Lord make him like his dear grandfather. We have long desired a young Philip Henry, if God please; but, methinks, I would rejoice with trembling, as in all other my comforts. When I see how many ministers' children prove a blemish to that high and holy calling, I fear and tremble, lest any of our's [sic] should prove so.

Philip never married, and died in 1760 leaving a fine country house, Hefferston Grange, in Weaverham, Cheshire.

New meeting-house

Around the turn of the century there were also some encouraging new developments for Matthew in his ministry at Chester. The work had grown and the old meeting-place at White Friars was now proving to be rather inconvenient. In addition, Anthony Henthorn, the owner of the property, was no longer with them, having moved to Ireland around 1692, and his son died in 1695. His grandson was not so sympathetic to their cause, so it was agreed to purchase a plot of land to build a chapel to house the people who attended. As a result of the freedoms obtained under the Toleration Act of 1689 it was becoming common for dissenters to erect more obvious places of worship. A site was obtained in Crook Lane, just off Watergate Street, near Trinity Church, and the foundation stone laid in September 1699. The cost of building the new place of worship came to over £532. A list of those who contributed to the cost indicates that 242 people gave an amount that totalled just over £491. The remaining shortfall was soon cleared. It was John Hulton, his late sister Ann's husband, who had the responsibility of collecting the money and paying for the work to be done. Matthew was well pleased with the new building and commented later: 'It is very commodious, capacious, pleasant place, and many a comfortable Day we have had in it. Blessed be God.'

It was on 8 August 1700 that the congregation gathered for the opening service, when Matthew preached from Joshua 22:22–23: 'The LORD God of gods, the LORD God of gods, he knoweth, and Israel he shall know; if it be in rebellion, or if in transgression against the LORD … that we have built us an altar.' This may sound a most unusual text for such an occasion; but as indicated by the title that the preacher gave it, namely, 'Separation without Rebellion', Matthew was well aware of the prejudices and misconceptions entertained by those belonging to the established church. Despite the Toleration Act, it was still a sensitive issue and many of Chester's citizens and Anglican clergy would have been none too pleased with this new dissenting meeting-house for worship. It was also for this reason that the sermon was not published during Matthew's lifetime. Isaac

Watts, the hymn-writer, wrote a commendatory preface when it appeared in print in 1726.

On the first Sunday in September of that year, when they held the first communion service in the new building, his sister Sarah was present. She commented:

> I had a comfortable day joining with that assembly in holy ordinances. In the forenoon, brother went on in expounding gospel Psalms, such as especially look at Christ... We had the Sacrament of the Lord's supper—the first in the new chapel— administered, which I have often found sweetness in. I received a pardon as being the purchase of that precious blood which purchases precious privileges, and nourishes precious graces and comforts. Lord, evermore give me of this bread.

Harvey's congregation

Under Matthew's ministry the congregation in Crook Lane continued to grow, so that in May 1707 it was necessary for a gallery to be added in the chapel. Matthew reckoned that there were by then over 350 communicants. In large part, the increase was due to John Harvey's flock joining them. Old Mr Harvey had died quite suddenly in November 1699 and there was clearly some concern over what would happen to his congregation and whether they should amalgamate with Matthew's. It was a delicate situation for Matthew, who had always been very careful in his associations with the old minister to gain his confidence and support ever since he had been called to Chester. He did not wish to cause more trouble with any precipitous action. Matthew wrote in his diary: 'As to the disposal of the congregation, I have solemnly, and with the greatest indifference, referred it to God; resolving to be purely passive, and earnestly begging that it may be so ordered, as may redound most to his glory, and the furtherance of the gospel in this place.' In the event, Harvey's congregation chose his son Jonathan to succeed him and he was ordained a Presbyterian minister at Warrington in 1701. By 1706 Harvey's congregation began to dwindle and by the beginning of the following year Jonathan resigned through ill health. He was only thirty years old when he died of tuberculosis in 1708.

It was an embarrassing position for Matthew, but through the whole episode he was careful to act in a way that was above reproach. Harvey's congregation had actually been voting with their feet for some time, moving over to him in dribs and drabs. This is how he wrote about the whole affair:

> I have had many searchings of heart about Mr. Harvey's congregation who come dropping in to us. As I have endeavoured, in that matter, to approve myself to God, and my own conscience; and my heart doth not reproach me; so, blessed be God, I hear not of any person, one or other that doth.

In fact, he had been experiencing some difficulties among his own people. Alderman Mainwaring was no longer attending and his wife was a particular discouragement to Matthew. The temptation for ministers to give up their preaching and pastoral work can be very strong, especially when people of promise disappoint, church discipline proves futile, and they become mouthpieces of Satan. Matthew quotes the Lord's Servant: 'Then said I, I have laboured in vain, and spent my strength for nought' (see Isaiah 49:4) and added: 'These things are a temptation to me to lay aside the pastoral charge, but I dare not. I cannot do it.'

Matthew admitted in his diary that 'Providence so ordered it that Mr. Harvey's congregation are generally come in to us, or else we began to dwindle, so that I should have gone on very heavily.' But he also knew what every minister with discernment is aware of, that numbers are not everything, and he did not rest content with additions by transfer from elsewhere. His desire was to see the congregation grow spiritually, that the 'word of the Lord might prosper among them'. Over the next few years he saw answers to his prayers with 'many' converted and becoming members of the household of faith.

9

Wider ministry

Besides the work in his own church, Matthew had been engaged, almost from the beginning, in preaching to the prisoners in Chester castle. It was the jailor's wife who seems to have been instrumental in bringing this need to the attention of Matthew. She was a godly lady, deeply concerned about the eternal destiny of those who were incarcerated. For nearly twenty years Matthew faithfully visited the prison and preached to the inmates. He himself was moved by the condition of those so obviously dead in sins and feeling nothing of the awful doom that awaited them beyond this world. He said of such people that their 'peace is like the sleep of a man in a lethargy: it is not peace—but senselessness and stupidity. They love darkness and sit in it. My heart bleeds for them. Men are destroyed for lack of knowledge.' In a letter to his wife, who was staying with her parents at the time, Matthew mentions how he had been 'spending some time this morning with the poor man that is to be hang'd this afternoon. 'Twas a melancholy thing to hear him give orders for the making of his own grave.'

Matthew encouraged these poor wretches to turn to the Lord and know salvation in Christ, using Old and New Testament passages in his messages. He spoke to them about Manasseh's repentance when he was imprisoned (2 Chronicles 33:12), reminding them that 'There is a way that seems right to a man, but its end is the way of death' (Proverbs 14:12, NKJV). By warning and pleading from such texts as Proverbs 14:9; Ecclesiastes 9:5; and Leviticus 26:23–24, he encouraged his hearers that their imprisonment could turn out for their good as Psalm 119:67 indicated: 'Before I was afflicted I went astray, but now I keep your word' (NKJV). He urged them to flee from the wrath to come 'when the Lord Jesus is revealed from heaven … in flaming fire taking vengeance on those who do not know God, and on those who do not obey the gospel of our Lord Jesus Christ' (2 Thessalonians 1:7–8, NKJV). Other texts Matthew used were taken from Jeremiah 3:21; Luke 12:5; and James 1:15. These evangelistic sermons were brought to a stop by a local Anglican curate, upset that a Nonconformist was engaged in this ministry. He pressed the governor of the prison to discourage the practice and eventually Matthew's services were terminated; but not before he preached his last sermon there concerning the penitent thief on the cross from Luke 23:39–43.

Nominal Christians

Matthew Henry's concern for the lost was not confined to those who seemed beyond hope of reformation. He was likewise grieved at the state of so many who professed Christianity. This was noticeable by the end of the seventeenth century among a growing number with Presbyterian leanings as well as many within the national church. He writes:

> There are but few who are truly religious; who believe the report of the gospel, and who are willing to take the pains, and

run the hazards of religion. Many make a fair show in the flesh, but few only walk closely with God. Where is he that engageth his heart, or that stirs up himself to take hold of his Maker?

It was often accepted that if people could say the Lord's Prayer and the *Apostles' Creed* or recite the catechism they were accepted as professing Christians. Matthew was concerned for their true spiritual condition. While it was common to be troubled, and rightly so, over the condition of the materially poor in society, Matthew was disturbed that there was no similar concern over the spiritually ignorant. This is how he put it: 'It is our common complaint that there are so many poor, but who complains that there are so many ignorant, which a man may be, and yet be able, like a parrot, to say his creed and catechism. Those who knew not the way of the Lord, yet said, "the Lord liveth". Matthew's concerns were those of a former generation of Puritans. His age cared more about reason, morality and science than inner spiritual transformation.

Other congregations

Matthew Henry's time at Chester involved him in caring for churches over a wide area of Cheshire and Shropshire as well as over the border into Wales at Broad Oak and Wrexham.

There were many calls on his services from near and far. Hardly a week went by that he was not ministering in some village or town close by. Within a distance of ten miles to the north east or south east of Chester he held monthly lectures (that is, preaching meetings) in villages like Bromborough on the Wirral, Elton and Moulsworth (near Helsby), and Saighton (near Chester); and even more frequently in places like Mickledale, near Helsby, Burton, near Tarvin, and further toward Beeston and Peckforton, and to Darnal, near Winsford. Beyond the county of Cheshire he made frequent visits into North Shropshire to the market towns of Whitchurch and Wem, the villages of Boreatton and Prescott, near Baschurch, and further south to Shrewsbury. Matthew often administered the Lord's Supper at Boreatton. This was where Roland Hunt, a Presbyterian of the landed gentry, lived and where Matthew's father, Philip Henry, had been a frequent guest. In these travels he would normally call at Broad Oak, the family home, and at Wrenbury Wood near Nantwich, where his sister Sarah lived with her husband and children. At both these places he was often invited to preach to the people who met there before travelling further.

Once a year he made visits to Nantwich, Newcastle-under-Lyme and sometimes to Stafford and Market Drayton. During March 1705 at Stone, seven miles south of Stoke-on-Trent, Matthew preached at the opening of a new meeting-place, taking as his text Psalm 101:2. Other annual journeys to minister God's Word took him to Manchester, Stockport, Bolton, Warrington and Liverpool.

'Happy Union'

Matthew was a strong advocate of closer ties with other Protestant dissenting ministers. Various piecemeal attempts had been made between Presbyterians and Congregationalists in different parts of the country to establish joint meetings; but a more formal union became more feasible with the failure of the Comprehension Bill of 1689. The Presbyterians had hoped that the bloodless Glorious Revolution of 1688 would have enabled them to be part of a wider national church that would allow for their sincerely held differences over church government to be accommodated. But there were too many opposed to the idea. It meant that the Presbyterians were forced into independency like the Congregationalists and the Baptists, which is the position they had in fact been in since the Act of Uniformity of 1662. It eventually led to John Howe (1630–1705), a leading Presbyterian minister, pressing for greater co-operation with the Congregationalists and eventually 'Heads of Agreement' were signed by almost all the Presbyterian and Congregational ministers in London on 6 March 1691. This so-called 'Happy Union' was formally inaugurated at the Stepney meeting-house a month later, when the minister preached on 'the two sticks made one' from Ezekiel 37:19. The dissenting ministers in the rest of the country were encouraged to adopt the agreement and, along with many other areas, the Cheshire Union, to which Matthew Henry belonged, was formed that same year. They met twice a year, in May and August, Knutsford being the main location for the meetings. While the 'Union' in London turned into a short, unhappy affair, the association of ministers in Cheshire and some other places continued for many years.

The Cheshire fraternal of ministers met to pray together, to hear the Word preached, to share experiences about pastoral issues in their churches, to discuss any difficulties arising over the admission or suspension of church members and to give help and advice to ministers contemplating moving to another pastorate. One matter off the agenda at all times was any discussion relating to the established church and the state. Such gatherings of ministers also provided an opportunity for ministerial students to be examined and ordained. Matthew refers to many such ordinations in his diaries and it is quite impossible at times to know whether they were Congregational or Presbyterian men. They did not all take place at the Knutsford fraternals. In fact, they often occurred in villages and towns over a wide area, including Macclesfield in 1700, Warrington in 1702 (where Jonathan Harvey, old Mr Harvey's son, was ordained), and Winslow and Nantwich in 1707. The candidates on these occasions came from as far away as Newmarket (now called

Trelawnyd) near the North Wales coast, Knighton in Mid Wales and Kendal in the Lake District. Some were settled in ministries equally distant from where they were ordained, in places like Ashby-de-la-Zouch in Leicestershire, the cathedral city of Lichfield in Staffordshire and Leominster in Herefordshire.

Two ordinations were of particular interest to Matthew Henry. The first took place in January 1699. There was only one candidate, Samuel Benyon (1673–1708), who had been Philip Henry's assistant and was now being ordained to succeed to the pulpit of the late venerable preacher. Interestingly, the ordination was held at Broad Oak, Matthew's old home, where Benyon was to be the minister. In addition, whereas previously Matthew Henry had declined being actively involved, believing that for such solemn events the older ministers should take the lead, for this special occasion he reveals, 'I could not decline'. There was disappointment that Francis Tallents of Shrewsbury was not able to be present due to failing health; but included in the number of ministers were some of Matthew's friends, Samuel Lawrence of Nantwich, Richard Latham (d. 1706) of Wem, and James Owen.

As was the recognized practice among the Presbyterians, on the first day Benyon, a graduate of Glasgow University, 'was examined in the languages, and philosophy', and defended a thesis in Latin on 'whether a divine revelation were necessary for the salvation of fallen man'. Matthew remarked: 'We rejoiced in his great abilities'. The public meeting took place the following day, which was kept, as usual, as a fast day, when a good number gathered. After prayer, an account of what the meeting was about and the singing of a psalm, Matthew Henry preached from Isaiah 6:8: 'Here am I; send me', and closed in prayer. James Owen, the moderator, then called for the candidate's confession of his faith and ordination vows, which satisfied all the ministers present. Benyon was then set apart, the normal practice being for the ministers to lay hands on him, and the moderator concluded the proceedings with a suitable word of exhortation. 'We have reason to say it was a good day, and the Lord was among us,' wrote Matthew. From then on Matthew took part in many such ordinations sometimes preaching, sometimes praying, at other times acting as moderator or examining the candidates.

The second ordination that was of special interest to Matthew was one that took place at Whitchurch. Again there was only one candidate, who had been called to the Whitchurch chapel. Matthew's love and concern for the spiritual welfare of this company of worshippers is made clear both in his private diaries and in his final exhortation to the congregation after the ordination. He commented: 'I cannot *but* have a love to *that* people in particular'. Many of them belonged originally to the congregation which had met at Broad Oak during his father's ministry. When Samuel Benyon, who had by then obtained qualifications as a medical doctor, left Philip Henry's congregation in 1706 for Shrewsbury, the Broad Oak congregation moved to an area of Whitchurch called Dodington where most of the worshippers lived, and there started building a meeting-house despite much opposition. The following year the building was opened and Matthew preached on Matthew 18:20: 'Where two or three are gathered together in my name, there am I in the midst of them'. While they were without a regular minister Matthew visited them often and on one occasion preached and celebrated the Lord's Supper.

In April 1712 he presided as moderator at the ordination of another Benyon (there were many families with that name in the locality). This Benyon had been of considerable help to the Dodington church and the people were pleased to call him as their minister. Matthew saw it as a wonderful answer to prayer. This young man acquitted himself well, having been assigned by Francis Tallents a thesis with the title, 'The righteousness by which we are justified before God is the righteousness of Christ the Mediator'. This strongly suggests that the theology of the ministers associated with Matthew Henry was still the traditional Protestant and Reformed teaching as taught by John Owen rather than the views propagated by Richard Baxter.

Division

One place, eleven miles from Chester, where the events which brought the ill-fated 'Happy Union' to an ignominious end had local repercussions and where Matthew Henry was forced to take sides, was at Wrexham. This town was the largest in Wales at the time and had been a centre of Puritan activity from Elizabethan days. During the Commonwealth period of Oliver Cromwell, Morgan Llwyd was the official non-episcopal minister at the parish church as well as of a group of Congregationalists, some of whom had Baptist leanings. Shortly before the Restoration of the monarchy, Matthew Henry's father had turned down a call to become the minister of Wrexham parish church, but he maintained a strong link with those who refused to conform and throughout his ministry at Chester and until his death, Matthew Henry was a frequent and much appreciated preacher to the sizeable congregation that met there.

The disagreement that finally split the 'Happy Union' arose in large measure over a theological dispute between two Welshmen. One of Wrexham's most outstanding Nonconformist sons, Dr Daniel Williams (1643/4–1716) of Dr Williams's Library fame, who was by then minister of Hand Alley church in London and a prominent leader among the Presbyterians, accused Richard Davis, a fiery but tactless South Wales preacher who had become the minister of the Congregational church at Rothwell, Northamptonshire, with being an Antinomian (a person who believed that the moral law was not applicable to those justified by faith alone). While some Congregationalists admitted there was some truth in the allegation, others rallied to Davis's side. The outcome was that Presbyterians denounced Congregationalists as Antinomians (stressing freedom from God's law leading to sinful presumption) and Congregationalists denounced Presbyterians as Arminians (stressing human responsibility to the detriment of God's sovereignty) and even worse, Socinians (denying the Trinity and deity of Christ). The Independents of Wrexham took sides over the issue and before 1691 was over, the Presbyterians and some Congregationalists withdrew and formed 'The New Meeting', leaving most of the Congregationalists and Baptists at the 'Old Meeting'. Matthew Henry sympathized with the seceders and helped them until they found a minister. About the year 1700, Daniel Williams gave money for the building of a chapel and Matthew was one of the trustees. It was to this congregation that Matthew preached as much as twice a month and in his diary for 21 May 1706 he includes this note: 'Went to Wrexham … preach'd the Lecture there Zech. 1.5. After Sermon baptized publickly Hannah the daughter of Simon Edwards.'

Death of Matthew's mother

One particular sadness within the family occurred during this time. In Matthew Henry's review of 1705, among the items he listed for which he was thankful he mentions that his children had survived the smallpox, that his wife had been upheld under great weakness, and that his mother 'though brought low, has been helped'. Katharine Henry, by now a great age for those times, who had been slowly declining in health over the past year, quietly passed away early on Sunday morning, 25 May 1707 at the age of seventy-eight. Around the same period Mr Pell, who was then the minister, had been seriously ill with tuberculosis and old Mrs Henry had sent him a message a few weeks before she died which read, 'Desire Mr. Pell not to be angry if I get to heaven before him'. In the event, Pell died first, on the previous Wednesday!

While Matthew's wife and his two remaining sisters, Sarah and Katharine, were present at their mother's bedside when she died, he was in Chester, preparing for the Sunday ministry. He heard the sad news before entering the pulpit that morning and his diary reveals the difficulty he experienced in expounding the Scriptures to the people that day while at the same time very aware of his responsibilities: 'I endeavoured to do the work of the day in much weakness and heaviness, because Christ would not suffer him, whom he called to preach the gospel, to go first and bury his father'. As soon as the evening service was over he made his way 'to the beheaded family at Broad Oak, where we wept and prayed together'. The following two days were spent preparing for the funeral. Dr Samuel Benyon, her former minister and now at Shrewsbury, preached a moving sermon from Hebrews 6:12 at Broad Oak before her body was taken for burial beside her husband's remains in the parish church at Whitchurch.

In a funeral sermon for her, preached the following Wednesday on Proverbs 31:28: 'Her children arise up, and call her blessed', Matthew spoke affectionately of his mother:

> if ever any children in the world had reason to rise up and call a parent blessed, we have.—So wise, so kind, so tender, charitable, prudent, provident, and above all, so pious. Sure we can never say enough in her praises; all that knew her will with us bear record.

10

In demand

Matthew was ten years in Chester before he made any visit to London. But on Monday 2 May 1698 he set out with his friend William Tong, minister at Knutsford, Cheshire, preaching on the way at Nantwich, Newcastle-under-Lyme, Lichfield and Sutton Coldfield. Matthew was particularly keen to visit the latter place, for it was where the Puritan Anthony Burgess (d.1664) was rector until he was ejected in 1662. They reached London after paying a short visit to the Presbyterian minister, Jonathan Grew, at St. Albans. Matthew preached in the metropolis almost every day, being well received wherever he went. At a fast kept at John Howe's meeting place, he preached from an appropriate text for those times, Acts 28:22: 'a sect every where spoken against'. The sermon was later published.

Before he made a further visit to London in 1704 there had been a change of sovereign. The co-regency of William of Orange and Mary lasted until Mary died in 1694. Her husband reigned alone until his death in 1702, when Mary's younger sister, Anne, the last of the Stuarts, succeeded to the throne.

Queen Anne's London was an impressive place. No other place in Britain came anywhere near it in terms of size and population. There had been many changes since Matthew was a student in the city. He would have noticed the many new buildings on London Bridge and the newly erected parish churches designed by Christopher Wren, with the massive Cathedral of St Paul's still under construction. The port, too, had greatly expanded to become an international trading centre.

Matthew took his wife with him on this occasion. No doubt he showed her some of the tourist attractions that had impressed him on his first visit as a student. Matthew records how he heard John Howe preach from Jude 21. What stuck in Matthew's mind were the preacher's words, 'I would deal for your souls, as for my own, and for myself I declare before you all, I depend purely upon the mercy of our Lord Jesus Christ for eternal life.' Matthew was clearly encouraged that Howe was emphasizing the traditional gospel truths over against those who were preaching a new legalism.

Early writings

By this time Matthew had become well known as much through his writings as his preaching. His first published work was *A brief inquiry into the true nature of schism*, which appeared in 1690. It resulted in two anonymous pamphlets scurrilously attacking what appeared to many to be a very balanced and gracious production. His friend William Tong came to his defence with well-written replies. In 1694 Matthew produced a 'collection of family hymns from various authors' including a short essay on psalmody. A second edition appeared in 1702 'with large additions'. It was, however, the publication of a biography of his father, Philip Henry, in 1698 that brought his name to wider public attention. *A Scripture Catechism* was published in 1702 (later translated into Welsh), and *A Plain Catechism for Children* appeared the following year. Besides a couple of sermons published in 1705, a work that was to prove popular was his *The Communicant's Companion*. This, along with the life of his father, was presented to Queen Anne by Sir Henry Ashurst (1645–1711), a friend of the Henry family. In Matthew Henry's diary for 8 May 1708 he remarked: 'Wrote to Sir H. Ashurst, who writes me, that, last Saturday, he presented the Queen [Anne] my father's Life, and my book of the Sacrament;—sapless things, I fear, at court, and, I am sure, unworthy to be so regarded.'

Calls

Recognizing his pastoral heart and warm, earnest preaching, other churches began to invite Matthew to become their pastor. When Dr William Bates, the ejected vicar of the London parish of St Dunstan's in the West, and afterward the first minister of the dissenting congregation at Hackney, died in 1699, Matthew declined the call to succeed the influential 'silver-tongued' preacher and renowned scholar. Again, on the death of their minister, Nathaniel Taylor, who had served them from 1695 to 1702, the Presbyterian congregation in Salters' Hall Meeting House, Cannon Street, London, invited Matthew to take his place. This call to such a prestigious position came with accompanying persuasive letters from leaders of the calibre of John Howe and Daniel Williams. This naturally concerned Matthew for some time as to how he might discern the Lord's will, especially as several members of his church, hearing of this very attractive offer, earnestly entreated him not to leave them. In the end he turned down the invitation.

Matthew later indicated his thoughts on the whole issue: 'The invitation to the congregation at Salter's Hall was a surprise to me. I begged of God to keep me from being lifted up with pride by it ... Had I consulted either my own fancy, which had always a kindness for London ever since I know it, or the worldly advantage of my family, I had closed with it; and I was sometimes tempted to think it might open a door of greater usefulness.' Though he believed that 'ministers married to their ministry', he could see no scriptural grounds for believing that ministers are 'married to their people'. But among the reasons that persuaded him to refuse the tempting offer were fears concerning his own fitness for the work, the natural concerns over moving to a new and unknown place and work, and above all the mutual affection that existed between him and his Chester congregation which he did not want to see severed in any way.

In 1705 another request came, this time from Manchester; and then a further invitation from London in 1708 to accept a joint pastorate with the celebrated John Shower (1657–1715), who had an ever-growing congregation in the heart of the city at Old Jewry. Matthew declined both offers on account of his love for the people of Chester. Remarking on his refusal to accept the Manchester proposition he wrote: 'I cannot think of leaving Chester till Chester leaves me.'

In September 1708 there was an even stronger pull for him to leave Chester for London. When John Howe's successor at Silver Street died, Matthew received numerous communications from friends and eminent ministers like William Tong and Daniel Williams to accept the call that the church had given him to be their pastor. The church was not easily deterred by Matthew's refusal but made repeated attempts, including financial incentives, to persuade him to change his mind. William Tong could write to Matthew in February of the following year:

'The whole city, from Westminster to Wapping, seems very heartily to wish, and long for your coming.'

During this time of uncertainty and continued pressure to consider a move to London, Matthew received numerous poison-pen letters. In one derisive note the anonymous author remarked that he would not have Matthew go to London for he would do more mischief there than at Chester. In his distress and confusion Matthew Henry decided to contact Dr Edmund Calamy (1671–1732), the Nonconformist theologian and historian and arranged a meeting with him as he journeyed back to London from his grand tour of Scottish universities, where he received the degree of Doctor of Divinity. Later, Matthew received a considered response from Calamy that took account of all Matthew's misgivings and urged him to reconsider the invitation. Yet, even Calamy's letter failed to persuade him, so close was Matthew's attachment to the Chester congregation.

Further publications

All these invitations and persuasive letters from the leading Presbyterian preachers of London to minister in the metropolis indicate how well respected Matthew Henry had become. By 1710 his abilities as a writer and preacher were appreciated even more. As a result of his 1704 visit to London, some of those who belonged to The Society for the Reformation of Manners encouraged him to publish the following year his *Four Discourses against Vice and Profaneness.* Other published sermons followed: *Great Britain's present Joys and Hopes* in 1707, and various funeral sermons between the years 1706 and 1708 for long-standing friends and fellow ministers like James Owen, Dr Samuel Benyon and Francis Tallents. Appended to the latter two were short accounts of their lives. In 1710 another work that proved very popular and of great spiritual profit was *A*

Method for Prayer, with Scripture Expressions proper to be used under each head. Isaac Watts, the well-known early hymn-writer, considered it a 'judicious collection of scriptures proper to the several parts of that duty'.

During the first decade of the new century Matthew began the work that was to bring about his world-wide fame in Christian circles. His popular commentary began life as a way of engaging his mind and using his spare time in an enjoyable way. When a commentary by William Burkitt (1650–1703), a Church of England vicar, appeared entitled, *Expository Notes with Practical Observations on the New Testament* (the Gospels in 1700 and Acts to Revelation in 1703), his friends urged Matthew to attempt something similar on the Old Testament to complement Burkitt's work. The first five books of Moses were published in 1706, Joshua to Esther two years later, Job to Song of Solomon in 1710 and the final books of the Old Testament in 1712.

Indecision and distress

After Matthew's initial refusal in 1699 to become the pastor of the Hackney congregation, the church had called Robert Billio, the son of an ejected minister, to succeed Dr William Bates. In May 1710 Billio died from smallpox and a fresh letter of invitation arrived for Matthew the following month, informing him that they had 'unanimously chosen me to be their minister'. As before, Matthew Henry dismissed the approaches; but like the importunate widow the church kept on pressing him, adamant that they would not accept a negative reply. In the end he decided to meet them and after a couple of visits during July and August he agreed to spend longer with them the following spring. His hope was that they would lose interest and find someone else. But they agreed to his terms and in 1711 he was with them from May until the end of July. Before leaving, he indicated his acceptance of their invitation and that he would become their minister the following spring. Many of the London ministers had again advised him that 'for greater good, and a more extensive usefulness, that I should remove to Hackney'. The 'Minutes of the Cheshire Ministers' indicate that Matthew had shared his concerns with them throughout every stage and that they supported him in the decisions he made.

The whole affair caused Matthew much grief and heart-ache. Even when he had agreed to go, he had little peace of mind, begging God 'to incline my heart that way which should be most for his glory'. Having set down previously reasons for remaining in Chester he now wrote down the reasons for accepting the call to Hackney so that in the future he could be assured that he had not done it rashly. Among the eleven reasons he listed he mentions that the invitation was not only unanimous but importunate, that there would be 'a much wider door of opportunity to do good, opened to me at London, than is at Chester, that in publishing his *Expositions* he would be more conveniently near the press, that so many different ministers and friends had been united in their advice to accept the call, and significantly he adds that though many loved and valued his ministry in Chester, he had known such discouragement as to believe that his work there was done: 'many that have been catechized with us, and many that have been long communicants with us, have left us, and very few have been added to us.'

Having made this crucial decision to move to Hackney, he indicates in his diary that he endured much mental anguish from certain members of the Chester congregation when they learned that their minister was leaving. While there were those who appreciated his reasons for moving and continued to show him affection, there were others, some of whom he least expected, who expressed anger and treated him with disrespect. He needed a great deal of wisdom and grace to act with a meek spirit and keep his own emotions under control.

At the end of 1711 concerns over his decision to move were still worrying him, as his diary reveals: 'I have upon my knees, in secret acknowledged to the Lord that I am in distress, in a great strait. I cannot get clear from Chester; or if I could, cannot persuade myself cheerfully to go. I cannot get clear from Hackney, or if I could, I cannot persuade *uxorem meam* ['my wife'] cheerfully to stay.' On his last Sunday at Chester he wrote: 'A very sad day. O that by the sadness of their countenances and mine, our hearts may be made better … I see I have been very unkind to the congregation who love me too well.' When he finally arrived at Hackney there was still obvious uncertainty as to whether he had made the right choice, for we read, 'Lord *am I in my way?* I look back with sorrow for leaving Chester; I look forward with fear: but unto thee I look up.'

11

Hackney

At the beginning of the eighteenth century, Hackney was still a village on the northern outskirts of the City of London. The only dissenting place of worship at that time was the Presbyterian meeting-house in Mare Street, the congregation having first gathered under the ministry of Dr Bates in 1672. Surprisingly, there had been no substantial increase in numbers either under Bates or Billio, so that there were less than a hundred communicants when Matthew arrived, far fewer than those attending the Chester meeting. It was here that Matthew Henry commenced his ministry on Sunday 18 May 1712. He expounded Genesis 1 in the morning and Matthew 1 in the afternoon and also preached from the text, Acts 16:9: 'Come over into Macedonia, and help us'. But it was with a somewhat heavy heart that he preached, judging by the entry in his diary: 'An encouraging Auditory, O that Good may be done to precious Souls! But I am sad in Spirit, lamenting my Departure from my Friends in Chester; and yet if they be well provided for I shall be easy, whatever Discouragements I may meet with here.'

Busy ministry

During the short time he ministered in Hackney Matthew had very little time to himself. Besides the regular three Sunday services in his own congregation, he would often deliver an early Sunday morning lecture (exposition) at Little St. Helen's (now called St. Helen's Place, Bishopsgate) within the city walls, where a Presbyterian congregation had been gathering since 1672. Sometimes, after his own Lord's Day services, he would travel to other congregations meeting in places like Wapping and Rotherhithe to deliver evening expositions. During the week he was often employed two or three times a day in preaching in and around the London area.

In the September of his year of arrival at Hackney, Matthew journeyed to Dagnall Lane Chapel, St. Albans (where Spicer Street Congregational Church used to meet), and gave the concluding exhortation at the ordination of Samuel Clark (1684–1750). Dr Daniel Williams presided. This Samuel Clark, not to be confused with his near contemporary of the same name who was an influential Anglican clergyman, was to become an eminent Presbyterian theologian and pastor and special friend of Philip Doddridge. While he was there, Matthew took the opportunity to visit the former minister's widow, whom he had first met with her husband Jonathan Grew at St. Albans on his way from Chester to London in 1698. In his diary for that day strong feelings of nostalgia are evident when he writes:

> I visited Mrs. Grew; looked a sorrowful look towards Chester.

Work among the young and needy

Matthew Henry gave himself fully to the work to which he had been called. As at Chester, he saw the importance of giving special attention to instructing the young. As soon as he commenced his ministry in Hackney he set about catechizing the young people on Saturdays and was instrumental in a more general revival of catechizing in and around London by undertaking a catechetical lecture in London at the meeting-house that once belonged to his former tutor, Mr Doolittle. It proved to be very successful, and some testified that they owed their first spiritual impressions to the instruction they received at that time.

To encourage the work among the children of the poor, Matthew journeyed on New Year's Day 1713 south of the River Thames to Gravel Lane, Southwark, near to Shakespeare's Globe Theatre, to 'Mr. Marriot's meeting place, where there has been a charity school for twenty-five years; the only one among the dissenters.' He preached an anniversary sermon on the text 'Honour the Lord with thy substance' (Proverbs 3:9) and 'a collection was made amounting to about £35.' On another occasion he wrote: 'We lose what we save. Withholding that which is meet tends to spiritual poverty; the worst of all husbandry. It is like grudging seed to the ground.' From the text of Proverbs 3:9 he encouraged people to use their money to promote true religion in the places where they lived, to support and encourage the ministry, the education of the young, and the distribution of Bibles and other good books. What Matthew preached he practised. When a sizeable sum of money was given him he donated £20 to a charity school.

Robbers

His whole attitude to earthly possessions is revealed in his response to an incident that happened one Sunday evening as he was returning to Hackney from a preaching engagement in the city. His diary presents the time and circumstances.

1713. March 8th. Lord's-day. In the evening I went to London. I preached Mr. Rosewell's evening lecture, Psalm 89:16.—the joyful

sound. [Samuel Rosewell (1679–1722) was assistant to John Howe
and John Spademan at Silver Street, Cheapside, and preacher
of the lectures at Old Jewry Sunday evenings.] As I came home
I was robbed. The thieves took from me about ten or eleven
shillings. My remarks upon it were,—1. What reason have I to be
thankful to God, who have travelled so much, and yet was never
robbed before? 2. What a deal of evil the love of money is the root
of, that four men would venture their lives and souls, for about
half a crown a piece. 3. See the power of Satan in the children of
disobedience. 4. See the vanity of worldly wealth; how soon we
may be stripped of it. How loose, therefore, we should sit to it.

Health

In view of his parents' concerns over his health when he was
younger, it is remarkable how fit he was all through his Chester
ministry. He obviously did overexert himself when he first began
to preach, so that at the age of twenty-six he was laid low through
physical exhaustion. His concerned father, who knew from
his own personal experience all about 'pulpit sweat' and how
fervent preaching can sap the energy of the strongest, wrote him
a letter full of wise counsel and common sense. He urged him
to 'be careful of yourself, for prayers ought to be seconded with
endeavours.' Aware of his son's susceptibility to fevers, he advised:
'I think you should not, when you are warmed with preaching,
either drink small beer, which is an error on the one hand, or
sack [sherry], which is commonly offered, on the other; but both
together, not a full draught, but a little at a time; by degrees; and a
little warmed, not hot …'

When he was in his early forties, during August 1704, he was
reading a chapter of Scripture in the morning service when he
suddenly fainted. He recovered quickly and continued with
the service. Instead of taking a break, he fulfilled preaching

engagements some distance from Chester on the following two days, with the result that when he returned home he was forced to rest. It was the first time since he commenced his ministry in Chester that ill-health prevented him from occupying his pulpit on the Lord's Day. The fever lasted three weeks, but it did not prevent him from leading family worship each morning and evening.

Besides the exertion of preaching, travelling to fulfil his appointments was far from easy. It often meant riding on horseback to outlying towns and villages in all weathers. On returning to Chester from an ordination service in Wrexham late one August night in 1706, he fell from his horse but, thankfully, experienced no ill effects. All this wear and tear obviously took its toll on his physical frame; and during his time in Hackney he began to experience more frequent bouts of illness, including painful debilitating kidney stones and the effects of diabetes. He did not allow these ailments to keep him long out of the pulpit but pushed himself to the limits of his endurance. For instance, his diary records for Sunday 13 December 1713:

> This morning a little after midnight, I was seized with a fit of the stone; but blessed be God, the pain in about an hour went off; though fatigued with it yet the poor body was fitted in some measure to serve the Lord. I went to London, and preached the morning lecture at Mr. Robinson's from John xx.1: 'The first day of the week, early while it was yet dark.' I preached at Hackney, from Romans ii.8,9.

In his diary for 1 January 1714, as was his normal practice, he reflected on the past year. Besides the comments about his health, there is clearly a much more positive attitude toward his situation in Hackney. He is thankful for the many mercies received, 'a good measure of health; health in my family;

encouragement in my ministry, both in the congregation here, and at London ...'

New Testament Commentary

If he was not preaching to his own congregation and at other places, visiting the sick or conducting family worship, he was in his study praying, writing sermons, preparing manuscripts for the press and even reading and critiquing other men's scripts before their publication. In September 1712, not long after the commencement of his ministry in Hackney, Matthew began work on his New Testament commentary and completed the four Gospels and Acts by April 1714. A glance at his diaries during this period indicates how diligent and industrious he was in seeking to bring the whole project to a satisfactory conclusion.

> 1712. September 9. Began Matthew, but went in the morning to Salters' Hall, and stayed in town all day. 1713. February 10. Finished Matthew. 11. Began Mark. March 21. Mark xvi. Began Luke. July 10. Finished Luke. Began John. November 27. John xxi. Finished John to-day. Laus Deo [Praise be to God]. 28. Began to read over the Gospels. December 7. Read over John i. to vii. 11. Finished John.'

He continues:

> '1713. December 12. Began Acts, having st made an errand to the throne of grace for assistance. 1714. April 17. Finished Acts, and with it the 5th volume. Blessed be God that has helped me, and spared me. All the praise be to God. 19. Reviewed some of the sheets of the Acts. April 21. Began the Preface, but did little in it. 23. Studied the Preface. 24. Went on in the Preface.

While Matthew was engaged in this work, he was not unmindful of the renewed pressure to curb the influence of nonconformity in the country. A bill was introduced to plug a loophole in the Corporation and Test Acts. The Occasional Conformity Act received the royal assent in 1711. It prevented nonconformists as well as Roman Catholics from taking 'occasional' communion in the state church in order to become eligible for public office. In 1714 a further measure instigated by the Tories to stamp out dissent was the Schism Act, which would have prevented all non-Anglicans from educating their children in their own schools. Licences would only be granted to those who had received Holy Communion within the previous year. Matthew wrote a pamphlet about it entitled *Serious Thoughts about the Bill brought into the House of Commons against Dissenters' Schools, and Academies.* On 26 May 1714, along with Dr Daniel Williams and others, he appeared 'in the Court of Requests, against this wicked bill of persecution; but no good will be done.' He also went to Wapping to a day of prayer over the issue at which he preached from 2 Chronicles 20:12. As it happened, the day the Act was due to take effect, Queen Anne died, and it was never enforced. But by then Matthew's work on earth was over.

Chester visits

In order to encourage Matthew Henry to accept the call to be their minister, the Hackney congregation had suggested that for a few weeks each year he could return to preach in Chester and neighbouring churches. The first of these journeys he made from 20 July to 15 August 1713. He set out by the Chester coach to visit, as he puts it, 'my friends in the country, as I purposed, and promised when I came hither, aiming at God's glory, and the edification of souls.' On day three of his journey north-west, he reached Whitchurch, where many of his friends met him; and in the afternoon he went to his old home at Broad Oak and preached from Romans 1:11. The next day he went to Chester, where he had a warm welcome from friends in that city. Each

Lord's Day he preached at his old church and on the first Sunday of the month celebrated the Lord's Supper with 'my beloved flock; a great congregation.' On other days he ministered at Middlewich and at the gathering of ministers at Knutsford. As he prepared to journey back to Hackney, he spent a night with his sister Sarah and family, and preached at Whitchurch before saying goodbye to his friends there. Then he caught the coach to London and was happy to be back with his own family again. At the close of that year he records his thankfulness to God for 'the comforts of my journey to Chester' and for 'the happy settlement of the congregation there.'

Despite the increasing problems with his health, Matthew kept his commitment to the people of Chester and neighbourhood by visiting them again the following year. He set out on 31 May 1714 for what would be his last visit. His close ministerial associate, William Tong, accompanied him in the coach as far as St. Albans. Again he received a cordial welcome from his friends in Whitchurch and Chester. On the first Sunday in June he preached and celebrated the Lord's Supper at the Chester congregation, commenting afterward: 'I am here among my old friends, yet I find my new ones lie very near my heart among whom God has now cut out my work.' He was as busy as ever proclaiming 'the gospel of the grace of God' in Wrexham, Knutsford and Chowbent (now a part of Atherton, Greater Manchester). On his last two Sundays at Chester he preached from Hebrews 4 on the rest that remains for the people of God, warning the congregation in his final sermon that they should tremble with fear at the prospect of some failing to enter the promised rest. Little did the people realize he would so soon be at rest himself from his earthly labours.

12

Last journey

On Monday 21 June Matthew commenced his return journey to Hackney. He travelled first by horseback to Nantwich (on what is now the A51 road). Then the plan was to catch the London coach. He was clearly not well, although he intimated that he was all right, and a pharmacist friend commented before he left Chester that they would never see him again. Five miles into the journey he came to the village of Dudden and drank a glass of mineral water. As he neared Tarporley his horse stumbled and threw him. Those with him urged him to stop; but he insisted that he was not hurt and indicated his desire to continue to Nantwich, where he was booked to preach. In the large congregation waiting to hear him was his sister Sarah, who lived nearby, and she has given a full report of what happened that evening. Matthew's text was Jeremiah 31:18. Sarah commented that he was not his usual lively self in the pulpit, 'was something short, and afterwards, exceedingly heavy and sleepy'.

Also in the congregation was his close friend from teenage

years at Broad Oak, George Illidge. He had been instructed to conduct Matthew to the home of Sir Thomas Delves (1652–1727) after the meeting. In the event, Matthew became too unwell to go anywhere, so he was taken to the home of Samuel Lawrence's successor at Nantwich, Joseph Mottershead (1688–1771), who had studied for a year under Matthew Henry at Chester before ordination to the Presbyterian ministry. In his weakness Matthew requested his friends to pray for him, 'for now I cannot pray for myself'. He had a restless night, and the physician bled him. At about five o'clock he had a stroke that rendered him speechless and he died about three hours later on Tuesday morning, 22 June 1714.

The following day Sarah came to view the body of her dear brother commenting that 'there was nothing of death to be seen in his face, but rather something of a smile'. On Thursday John Reynolds (1667–1727), a Presbyterian minister from Shrewsbury, preached at Nantwich chapel from Matthew 25:21: 'Well done, good and faithful servant', and on Friday 25 June Matthew's bodily remains were taken to Chester. We read that when the procession reached the city, 'it was met by eight of the clergy, ten coaches, and a large company of horses; many dissenting ministers followed the mourners; and universal respect was paid by persons of note, and distinction'. There were sermons preached on the following Sundays in both Chester and Hackney, the preachers included Dr Daniel Williams and William Tong. Dissenting ministers throughout England and Wales mourned the passing of this godly, faithful preacher and Bible expositor.

Matthew's body was buried next to his first wife, Katharine, in the original medieval Trinity Parish Church in Watergate Street, the vicar at the time being on friendly terms with the family. This church was rebuilt in the nineteenth century and a small brass plaque with a Latin inscription was placed near the unmarked tomb. A tall granite obelisk with a bronze medallion portrait to the memory of Matthew Henry was unveiled in August 1860 in St. Bridget's churchyard, paid for by public subscription. Today, the area has been radically transformed and the monument stands in the centre of the busy grass-covered Grosvenor roundabout facing the Crown Court and Castle.

Very little is known of how Matthew's wife, Mary, was affected by her husband's sudden death; but she was left with a very young family to bring up. While Matthew's two eldest daughters, Katharine and Esther, were by then young women, Philip, their only son, was just fourteen, while Elizabeth was twelve, Sarah ten, Theodosia six and Mary three. Mary Henry died in August 1731 at the age of sixty-two.

Matthew's sister Sarah lived to a ripe old age. She died in 1752 in the home of her youngest daughter Hannah and her husband, who was a minister in West Bromwich. One Sunday in 1735 when she was feeling low her spirits were raised by finding a letter written by her brother fifty years earlier at the time of her wedding. To calm her fears at leaving her old home Matthew wrote: 'God is the same in all places. Christ is the same. The everlasting covenant the same. Get near the fountain; conscientiously improve the helps you have; and remember that Daniel and his fellows were in better liking with pulse and water, than all who did eat the portion of the king's meat.' It is one of many indications of his pastoral heart and biblical spirituality.

While the whole of his OT commentary in four volumes was published before his death, the fifth volume that covered the four Gospels and Acts, though completed before his death, was not published until 1721. The final volume contained his comments on the Epistles and Revelation, and was the work of ministerial friends, some of whom have already been mentioned, such as William Tong, John Reynolds and Samuel Rosewell, who made use of short-hand notes of his expositions to family and congregations by those who heard him. A Welsh summary of Matthew Henry's commentary was published in 1728, while a translation of the whole work in four volumes was produced during the years 1828 to 1835.

13

Legacy

Matthew Henry lived through times of great change in church and state. There was a general reaction both to the religious freedoms, moral rigours and Puritan doctrine and spirituality of the Commonwealth period. Furthermore, philosophers and churchmen were questioning the Bible's authority in the light of scientific advances. Reason was exalted, special revelation undermined and deism— the belief that included the idea of a machine-like universe originally created by God and operating so efficiently by the laws of nature that no divine intervention, such as miracles, was necessary—flourished. At the same time Socinianism became more attractive with its rejection of orthodox Christian theology concerning the Trinity, God's knowledge, predestination, Christ's pre-existence and propitiatory sacrifice, human nature and original sin.

Matthew came face to face with heterodox views when the notorious Thomas Emlyn (1663–1741), who did much to foster Unitarianism among the Dissenters, returned to England after his release from a Dublin jail in 1705. As he was passing through Chester he visited Matthew, who endeavoured to show him that 'even his own principles are nearer to the orthodox than the Socinian, which yet he was inclined to speak favourably of'. Then Matthew added: 'The Lord keep *me* in the way of truth'. Emlyn called on Matthew again two years later and his diary reads:

> I perceive he not only retains his corrupt opinions, but seems to me to speak favourably of deism. He tells me there are many deists; and he finds, in conversation, that they triumph in this— that when they meet with such as condemn them, they cannot get them to enter into a fair argument.

Matthew believed that pride in human reason was the cause of such heresy.

His beliefs

Matthew Henry followed in the footsteps of his Puritan father, holding firmly to the fundamentals of the Christian faith as set out in the Westminster Assembly's *Catechism*.

In the preface to his commentary on the Gospels and Acts, Matthew found it necessary to state his own convictions in the light of the attacks made upon orthodox belief. 'We live in an age', Matthew wrote, 'when Christianity and the New Testament are more virulently and daringly attacked' and Christ and his gospel 'ridiculed' not by the obvious enemies but 'by men that are baptized and called Christians'. To the so-called 'free thinkers' of his day Matthew made clear that they were not as free in their thinking as they thought: 'a secret enmity to a holy heavenly mind and life, forbid them all free thought; for so strong a prejudice have their lusts and passions laid them under against the laws of Christ that they find themselves under a necessity of opposing the truths of Christ, upon which these laws are founded'. To help those genuinely interested in considering the evidence, he refers them to Richard Baxter's *Reasons for the Christian Religion* and other apologetic works.

The Bible

For Matthew, the Scriptures of the Old and New Testaments were God's inerrant word. In the preface to the first volume of his commentary he refers to the work of the Holy Spirit in preparing the human authors and qualifying them to pen Scripture, not only putting it into their hearts to write but assisting their memories so that what they wrote was free 'from error and mistake; and what they could not know but by revelation, (as for instance, Gen. 1 and John 1) the same blessed Spirit gave them clear and satisfactory information of'. Atheists and deists are denounced in the strongest of terms 'with their vain-glorious pretensions to reason, as if wisdom must die with them', arguing that 'if the Scriptures be not the word of God, then there is no divine revelation now in the world, no discovery at all of God's mind concerning our duty and happiness'. In other volumes he continues to denounce the deists with their denial of divine revelation.

The gift of tongues he considers 'was one new product of the Spirit of prophecy' and given for a particular reason, that 'all nations might be brought into the church. These and other gifts of prophecy, being for a sign, have long since ceased and laid aside, and we have no encouragement to expect the revival of them; but, on the contrary, are directed to call the scriptures the *more sure word of prophecy*, more sure than voices from heaven; and to them we are directed to *take heed*, to search them, and to hold them fast, 2 Pet. i.19'.

God

The first chapter of Genesis, where the plural form of the word for God is first found, confirms for Matthew 'our faith in the doctrine of the Trinity, which, though but darkly intimated in the Old Testament, is clearly revealed in the New'. The three persons of the Trinity also 'consult and concur' in the formation of humans in the divine image and so are 'dedicated and devoted to Father, Son, and Holy Ghost. Into that great name we are, with good reason, baptized, for to that great name we owe our being.'

Humanity

Matthew believed that the God who made human beings has the right to rule over them by his law; that people are accountable to God; and that their happiness is bound up with knowing God's favour, which comes from doing what his law demands. But human nature is now unlike what it was when God first formed it. It is degenerate and in that state cannot please God. People stand guilty before a holy and righteous God and are totally incapable of rectifying the situation.

Way of salvation

Salvation from the guilt and power of sin and restoration to God's favour is by Jesus Christ, the mediator between God and humanity, as revealed in the New Testament. In the words of Matthew's confession:

> Here I see a proper method for the removing of the guilt of sin (that I may not die by the sentence of the law) by the all-sufficient merit and righteousness of the Son of God in our nature, and for the breaking of the power of sin (that I may not die by my own disease) by the all-sufficient influence and operation of the Spirit of God upon our nature.

The faith that justifies is receiving and embracing the divine revelation concerning the promised 'Lord Jesus the Mediator of the new covenant', as Matthew makes clear in his comments on Abraham. 'All believers are justified as Abram was', not by good works, even though he was so rich in them, but by faith. Such faith comes, 'not by thinking and seeing, as philosophy does, but by hearing, by hearing the word of God, Rom. x.17'.

Personal experience

As Matthew began his statement of belief, expressing himself in language appropriate to those impressed by reason and scientific evidence, he declared: 'the more freely I think, the more fully I am satisfied that the Christian religion is the true religion'. He closed his ten-point confession with these words:

> I cannot but think that the gospel of Christ has had some influence upon my soul, has had such a command over me, and been such a comfort to me, as is a demonstration to myself, though it cannot be so to another, that it is of God. I have tasted in it that the Lord is gracious; and the most subtle disputant cannot convince one who has tasted honey that it is not sweet.

Spirituality

Matthew Henry continued in that tradition of biblical piety that was a significant feature of Puritanism, which in turn owed so much to John Calvin and his writings on the subject. It was Matthew's first concern to have an ongoing relationship with God through Jesus Christ. His desire was to grow in holiness to the glory of God and to be an example of godliness to the people of God. A glimpse of Matthew's whole attitude can be seen in his diaries, especially on his birthday or at the beginning of a new year. Here is a typical example as he renews his covenant obligations:

This new-year's day I have solemnly renewed the resignation, and surrender of my whole self to God, as my God, deliberately and upon good considerations. I have renounced the world and the flesh, as knowing they cannot make me happy; and have devoted my whole self to the blessed Spirit … I, likewise, devote myself, through the Spirit, to the Lord Jesus Christ, as my Advocate with the Father, and my way to him; by him to be recommended to the grace and favour of God the Father, relying upon Christ's righteousness alone, for, without him, I am less than nothing, worse than nothing. I, likewise, devote myself, through the Lord Jesus Christ, to God the Father, as my chief good and highest end … O Lord, truly I am thy servant, I am thy servant; may I ever be free in thy service, and never desire to be free from it. Nail my ear to thy door posts, and let me serve thee for ever.

On his birthday in 1702 he writes:

This day I have completed the 40th year of my life; of life did I say? Rather, indeed, of my inactivity and folly, but of the tender mercy, kindness, and forbearance of God towards me. To Christ my Mediator I joyfully acknowledge myself a debtor for the supports, and aids, and comforts of life; and to that same Christ I wholly trust, that I shall receive from my God, wonderfully propitiated, the forgiveness of my sins, grace for seasonable help, and preservation even unto eternal life.

Prayer

For Matthew Henry, prayer was a most precious means of grace. On the last day of 1701 he records:

Believing prayer to be an instituted way of communion with God, and fetching in mercy and grace from him, I have comfort in it daily; my daily prayers are the sweetest of my daily comforts. Having of late had my body feasted above the ordinary meals, I desire this day to have my soul fed plentifully with the duty of prayer, and thus to close the year ...

Lamentation and humiliation head his list of 'errands to the throne of grace'. They include his own corruptions, the sins that hinder his spiritual progress, the defects in his ministerial work, his coldness in prayer. He bewails the little success he has had in his ministry, 'the miscarriages of some this year' and his grief that 'some of the young ones whom I have catechised and taken pains with are no comfort to me'. He grieves over the 'low condition of the church of God ... the protestant interest small, very small; a decay of piety; attempts for reformation ineffectual. Help Lord!' Prayer and supplication then follow for pardon of his sins and victory over temptations and the putting to death of his lusts; for the increase of his ministerial gifts; for the success of his labours, 'that sinners may be converted, saints built up, and the congregation flourish'; for the blessing of God on his wife and children. Each of these items is backed up by suitable scriptural verses. He also prays for other relations, friends, brothers in the ministry particularly in London, Dublin, Cheshire and Lancashire, for the congregation dear to his heart at Broad Oak and their minister, and finally for 'some Members of Parliament, and other gentlemen of my acquaintance'.

Family responsibilities

Matthew Henry can be criticized for not spending more time with his young family; but it would be unfair to suggest that he in any way neglected his duties toward them. He clearly had a deep love for his wife and children. In a letter to his wife when she was staying with her parents, he addressed her as 'My dear heart' and closed with 'Thine affectionately, M.H.' and expressed his longing for her to be home again. What he advised others to do he sought to carry out himself when he wrote: 'Do all you can to make your children love home.' Very aware that he could not force his children to be Christians, he did all in his power to inspire reverence and love for God. 'You cannot give them *grace*: that is God's gift: but duty is required. Children must be nursed for God, and our care should be that they may be pious.'

Unless he was ministering away, he led daily family worship, Sundays included, both morning and evening. After asking God's help he read from the Old Testament in the morning and the New in the evening, not necessarily a whole chapter at each sitting but about eight to ten verses, and then gave a few brief comments of explanation and practical help. A psalm was then sung followed by prayer and a blessing pronounced over his children, the whole taking about half an hour.

On Sundays after family worship at eight o'clock in the morning they would all gather for public worship. After dinner a psalm was sung and a short prayer offered and then Matthew would retire to his study until the afternoon congregation assembled. In the evening it was his policy to repeat at home the sermons he had given and many neighbours used to come to listen. There would be more singing and prayer, then the blessing was pronounced and the younger children catechized. After supper Psalm 136 was sung and the older children and servants were catechized. He listened to them repeat what they could remember of the sermons and the day concluded with prayer.

Conclusion

Matthew Henry was ever eager to give practical help to Christians beyond his immediate circle. This accounts for his two most significant works, that have been of such enormous benefit to the people of God for the past three hundred years. His commentary on the Bible is a gem and has been so reckoned by many prominent people, including preachers like George Whitefield, the Erskine brothers in Scotland and Charles Spurgeon, and more recently the theologian, James Packer. Students who require more detailed explanations of difficult texts are, in the preface to the first volume, referred to Matthew Poole's *Annotations on the Holy Bible* that had appeared toward the end of the seventeenth century. From his years of personal study of God's Word and sermon preparation, Matthew has given to the world a treasure of warm, devotional comment and practical wisdom that is often sprinkled with delightful, pithy, and sometimes witty remarks.

Matthew Henry's other significant work is *A Method for Prayer with Scripture Expressions proper to be used under each head*. As the title suggests, it encourages Christians to pray the way the Scriptures direct. Pleading the promises that God has made to his people excites faith in the God who is faithful to his Word and leads to earnest seeking after God, with a determination not to let go until he blesses. Matthew covers the five main elements in prayer: praise, confession, petition, thanksgiving and intercession. A further two chapters deal with prayers for particular occasions and ways of concluding prayer. There is wise pastoral advice on not spending so long alone in prayer that it becomes a burden instead of a privilege; and a reminder that there are other things that need to be done.

Matthew Henry's *Bible Commentary* and *Method for Prayer* bear witness to his lifelong appreciation of the importance of prayer and the ministry of God's Word in home and church life. Here is a legacy that churches, pastors, parents and individual believers can ill afford to ignore.

Bibliography

H. D. Roberts, *Matthew Henry and His Chapel 1662–1900* (Liverpool: The Liverpool Booksellers' Co. Ltd., 1901).

Matthew Henry Lee, *Diaries and Letters of Philip Henry* (London: Kegan Paul, Trench & Co., 1882).

J. B. Williams, *The Lives of Philip and Matthew Henry* (Edinburgh: Banner of Truth Trust, 1974).

J. B. Williams, *Memoirs of the Life and Character of Mrs. Sarah Savage* (London: Hallworth and Ball, 1829).

Further reading

Matthew Henry's *Complete and Unabridged Commentary on the Whole Bible*. (Various editions exist, or it can be downloaded free from the internet).

Matthew Henry's *A Method for Prayer* has been revised and edited by O. Palmer Robertson and entitled *A Way to Pray: A Biblical Method for Enriching Your Prayer Life and Language by Shaping Your Words with Scripture* (Edinburgh: Banner of Truth Trust, 2010). Another revised version can be downloaded free from the internet.

A sampler from Robertson's *A Way to Pray* is published by Banner of Truth in its 'Pocket Puritans' Series.